101 BASKETBALL REBOUNDING DRILLS

George Karl
Terry Stotts
Price Johnson

COACHES CHOICE

ISBN: 1-57167-080-7
Library of Congress Catalog Card Number: 96-71929

Book Layout: Michelle Summers
Cover Design: Deborah M. Bellaire and Julie L. Denzer
Diagrams: Michelle R. Dressen
          Antonio J. Perez
Developmental Editor: Joanna Wright
Cover Photos: Courtesy of the NBA
          Andy Haft

Coaches Choice Books is an imprint of: Sagamore Publishing, Inc.
                                           P.O. Box 647
                                           Champaign, IL 61824-0647
                                           (217) 359-5940
                                           Fax: (217) 359-5975
                                           Web Site: http//www.sagamorepub.com

CONTENTS

ACKNOWLEDGMENTS

The authors would like to thank John Sullivan for his editorial assistance in helping to write up drills presented in this book. The authors are also grateful for the professional assistance in publishing this book provided by the staff of Coaches Choice Books and Videos—particularly Michelle Summers, Joanna Wright, Debbie Bellaire and Julie Denzer.

Finally, special thanks are extended to all of the players and coaches with whom we have had the opportunity to work with over the years. Their efforts and feedback have helped influence the design and ultimately the selection of the drills included in this book.

DEDICATION

This book is dedicated to our families—who motivated us to strive for excellence and reach for new heights. Their love enriches and energizes us.

George Karl
Terry Stotts
Price Johnson

PREFACE

For the more than three decades that I have been playing and coaching basketball, I have observed countless situations on the court and literally thousands of individuals attempting to play the game to the best of their abilities. Collectively, my experiences have given me an opportunity to evaluate many techniques and fundamentals for playing competitive basketball and a variety of methods for teaching those techniques and fundamentals. In the process, I have come to realize that true learning occurs when there is a need to know, a solid understanding of how to learn exists, and coaches and players realize that a particular goal can be reached.

My co-authors and I wrote this book to provide basketball coaches at all competitive levels with a tool that can enable them to maximize the skills and attributes of their players. As a vehicle for teaching and learning, properly designed drills can have extraordinary value. Each of the four volumes of drills in this series features drills that I have collected, court-tested, and applied over the course of my coaching career. If in the process of using the drills presented in this book coaches are better able to develop the skills of their players, then the effort to write these drill books will have been well worthwhile.

George Karl

DIAGRAM KEY

G	— guard
PG	— point guard
SG	—shooting guard
F	— forward
SF	—small forward
PF	— power forward
C	—center

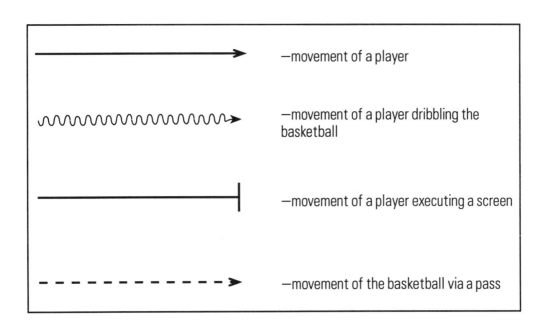

—movement of a player

—movement of a player dribbling the basketball

—movement of a player executing a screen

—movement of the basketball via a pass

CHAPTER 1

BASIC TECHNIQUE DRILLS

DRILL 1
SHAGGING THE SHOT

OBJECTIVE:
Develop basic rebounding skills.

DESCRIPTION:
Player #1 (P-1) shoots, and player #2 (P-2) rebounds. P-1 moves around the perimeter to shoot from a variety of angles and distances. Using either imaginary clear-out techniques or imaginary offensive rebounding methods, P-2 rebounds the shot and outlets the ball to P-1. After five shots, P-1 and P-2 rotate responsibilities (shooter to rebounder and vice versa).

VARIATIONS:
- P-1 shoots off the dribble.
- P-1 shoots off a pass from P-2.

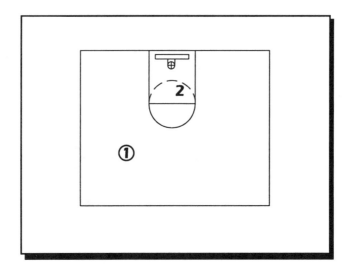

DRILL 2
TWO-LINE REBOUNDING

OBJECTIVE:
Practice basic rebounding skills.

DESCRIPTION:
The players divide into even-side lines, each side facing the basket. The drill begins with the first player in each line—player #1 (P-1) and player #7 (P-7) —with a ball. They throw the ball up on the backboard and rebound it. They then throw the ball back up on the board and go to the end of the opposite line. The new first players in line — P-2 and P-8 — repeat the actions of P-1 and P-7, by rebounding the ball, throwing it back up, and going to the end of the opposite line. The drill continues until every player has rebounded at least once from both lines. NOTE: While re-bounding, each player focuses on adhering to the proper techniques of rebounding, including ripping the ball to the chin and keeping the elbows out while rebounding, the feet spread and the head turned to the outside.

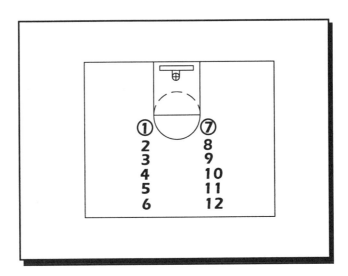

DRILL 3
SANDWICH TIME

OBJECTIVE:
To develop concentration while getting an offensive rebound.

DESCRIPTION:
Three players line up beside each other facing and in front of the basket. Player (0) is the middle player who is sandwiched between X-1 and X-2. (0) tosses the ball to the board so that it comes right back. (0) then goes right back up with the ball and attempts to score. The players on each side of (0) attempt to rebound the ball and prevent (0) from scoring. (0) is not allowed to dribble. Score is kept. Once (0) gets five rebounds, a new player is rotated into the middle (sandwich) position. Limited physical contact is permitted by the defenders.

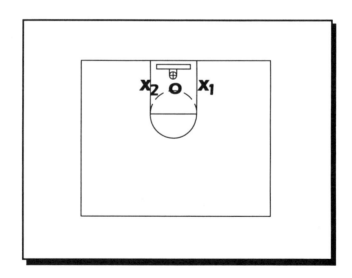

DRILL 4
ANTICIPATION

OBJECTIVE:
To teach players to anticipate when the ball is coming off the backboard after a shot.

DESCRIPTION:
The drill involves three players and two basketballs—one each with players P-1 and P-2. The drill is designed to make P-1 and P-2 anticipate where they need to be to rebound a shot taken by P-3. The drill begins by having P-3 v-cut and receive a pass from P-2. P-3 then shoots the ball, and P-2 rebounds the shot. P-3 v-cuts again and this time receives a pass from P-1. P-3 then shoots, while P-1 rebounds. The process is repeated a predetermined number of times as P-3 moves from side to side.

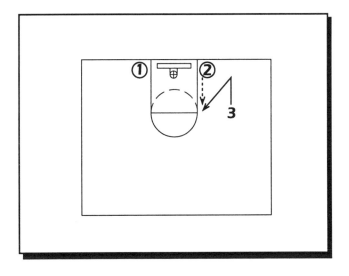

DRILL 5
THREE-MAN WEAVE

OBJECTIVE:
To develop lateral movement and footwork skills.

DESCRIPTION:
The drill involves three players and one basketball. The focus of the drill is to have players who do not rebound a shot in a given situation exchange positions with another player. Player P-1 shoots the ball off the backboard to P-3. P-1 and P-2 then interchange their positions. P-3, who now has the ball, puts it off the backboard to P-2. After making the pass, P-3 then interchanges positions with P-1. The drill continues for a predetermined number of interchanges or a period of time.

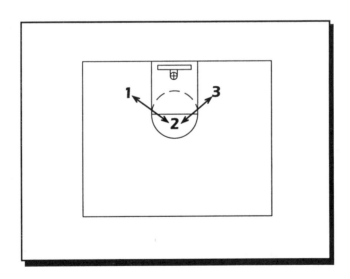

DRILL 6
POWER REBOUND

OBJECTIVE:
To develop balance and the ability to establish a sense of center of gravity.

DESCRIPTION:
The drill involves two players. The drill is initiated by having an offensive player (O) shoot the ball. When the defender (X) goes up to rebound the shot, the coach (C) applies additional physical force (e.g., a push) against (X) so that (X) is placed in a situation where (X) must focus on maintaining balance. The drill is designed to make defensive players concentrate on their center of gravity while rebounding.

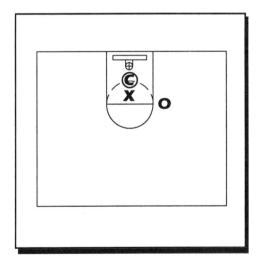 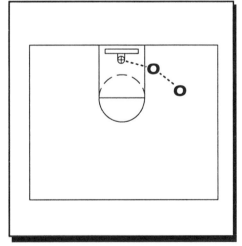

DRILL 7
TWO-ON-TWO REBOUNDING

OBJECTIVE:
Practice offensive and defensive rebounding techniques; develop court awareness and aggressiveness.

DESCRIPTION:
The drill involves both the coach (C) and two managers (M). The players divide into two equal-sized groups in a diagonal line facing the basket. The first player in each line is designated as a defensive player (X). The next player in each line is an offensive player (O). The defenders assume a defensive position. The drill begins when either the coach or a manager shoots the ball. Both offensive and both defensive players go for the rebound. If the shot is made, the steps are repeated with the same four players. If the shot is missed, the ball is rebounded. No follow up shots are taken by anyone. All players keep their own score. One point is earned for any rebound—offensive or defensive. The first player to earn five points is declared the winner. Rotation: offense to defense to the end of the opposite line.

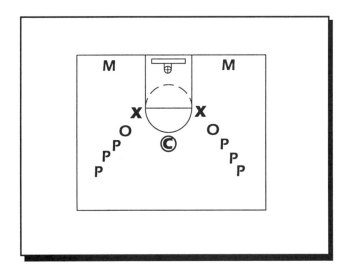

DRILL 8
THREE-PERSON REBOUNDING

OBJECTIVE:
Develop basic rebounding skills and on-court aggressiveness.

DESCRIPTION:
P-3 shoots, and both P-1 and P-2 go for the rebound. Whoever gets the rebound (either P-1 or P-2) then dribbles out at least 15 feet from the basket and shoots. The other two players contest for the rebound of the shot. If the shot is made, the shooter retains possession of the ball, and the steps are repeated. The drill continues for either a predetermined length of time or until a specific number of shots is taken.

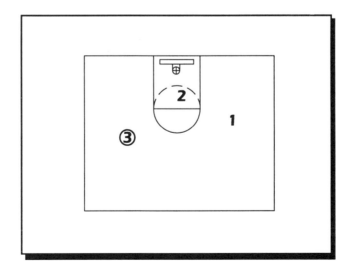

DRILL 9
ANTE-OVER

OBJECTIVE:
To practice rebounding techniques, footwork, tipping, and ball control.

DESCRIPTION:
The drill involves groups of three players at a basket. The middle player has a ball and starts the drill with a pass off the backboard (above the rectangle, which is over the rim) to the opposite player. The player receiving the pass tips the pass off the backboard to the player on the other side and then goes behind the player to whom the ball is tipped. The passer (initially the original middle player) assumes the position of the player who tipped the ball. The basic goal of the drill is to achieve continuous, controlled tipping by the group for a given number of repetitions.

COACHING POINTS:
- Players should keep their hands above their shoulders all of the time the ball is in play.
- Players should jump off of both feet and use two hands to capture the ball.
- Players should keep their elbows extended and use their fingers and wrists.
- Players should keep the ball above the rectangle and control the tip (catch and shoot the ball).
- The player tipping the ball should go behind the player to whom the ball is tipped.
- Each player should move quickly to the next spot; players should not slide and stare at the ball. Groups should be composed of players of equal size and jumping ability.

VARIATIONS:
- Players should first use either hand to tip.
- After players do well, they should be required to tip with their right hand when they're on the right side of the basket and their left hand when on the left side.
- Every player could be required to shoot a 1+1 after each rebound.

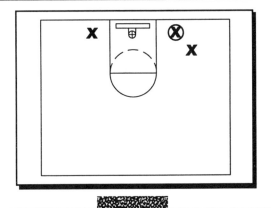

DRILL 10
THREE-PLAYER ANTE-OVER

OBJECTIVE:
To practice rebounding techniques and footwork.

DESCRIPTION:
The drill involves three players and one basketball. Player P-2 assumes a position in the lane, close to the basket. Players P-1 and P-3 take a position on the other side of the basket. The drill begins by having P-1 shoot the ball over the top of the basket to P-2. P-1 then moves to a position behind P-2. P-2 rebounds the ball and immediately shoots the ball back over the basket to P-3 and then moves behind P-3. P-3 shoots the ball to P-1, and the drill continues for a predetermined number of rebounds or a preset length of time.

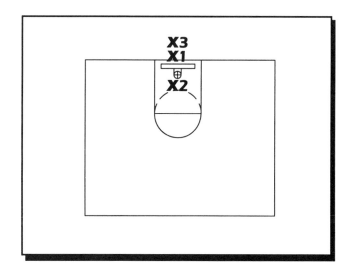

DRILL 11
GARBAGE TIME

OBJECTIVE:
To practice rebounding techniques and scoring moves.

DESCRIPTION:
Two lines of players form up on opposite ends of the free throw line facing the basket with a ball in each line. The first player in each line passes the ball off the backboard with a two-hand underhand toss. After rebounding the ball, that player then uses a predesignated scoring move to make a shot. Once the shot is made, the player passes the ball to the next player in line and then goes to the end of the opposite line.

COACHING POINTS:
- The coach should designate what offensive move the rebounder should use to score (e.g., tip overhead, power, lift, etc.)
- Players should be reminded that they should assume that every shot will be missed and has to be rebounded—until the ball goes into the basket.
- Every player should use proper rebounding form on every attempt. Players should have their hands up and jump quickly while rebounding. They should grab the ball with both hands and land in a solid base position with their heads held high and their legs locked. Players should hold the ball (which should never be brought below chest level) with their elbows out and their fingers up.

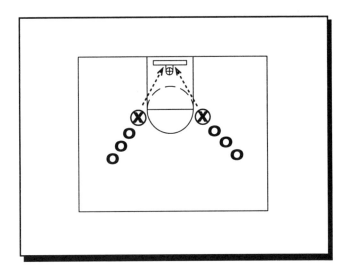

DRILL 12
REBOUND AND SHOOT WITH PRESSURE

OBJECTIVE:
To teach rebounding techniques, faking skills, and the ability to take the ball back up to the basket against pressure.

DESCRIPTION:
The drill involves one player acting as a rebounder, a manager (M) and the use of a machine (R) designated to facilitate the practice of rebounding techniques (NOTE: One of the most popular of these machines is simply called "The Rebounder"). If a rebounding machine is not available, the coach can shoot the ball off the backboard. The rebounding machine is set up close to the basket—preferably next to the rim of the basket. The drill is initiated by having the player pull (rebound) the ball from the rebounding machine. If a coach participates in the drill, the player takes the ball off the backboard. After retrieving the ball, the player immediately explodes back up to the basket and attempts to score. Simultaneously, the manager either brushes the player with a blocking dummy to increase the pressure on the player or places a tennis racquet in front of the player which simulates the requirement to shoot over outstretched hands.

VARIATION:
• Players can be required to use a fake before going back up to the basket.

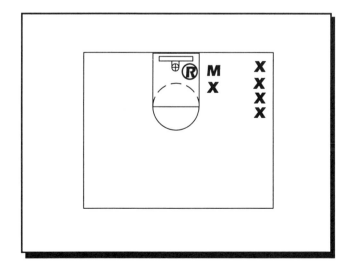

DRILL 13
REACTION REBOUNDING

OBJECTIVE:
To develop reaction skills, footwork, coordination, and rebounding techniques.

DESCRIPTION:
The players form a single line behind the foul line. Potentially obstructive objects (e.g., cones or chairs) are randomly placed in the foul lane. The coach (C) shoots the ball. The first player in line (X) must react to the shot, negotiate the objects, and get to where the shot will come off the backboard. The player must rebound the ball before the ball hits the floor. After rebounding the shot, the player goes strongly back up to the basket and attempts to score.

VARIATIONS:
- The cones can be arranged in a variety of ways.
- The coach can shoot from a variety of positions or use a variety of types of shots.

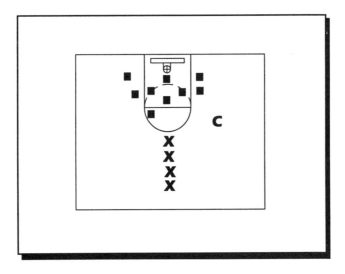

DRILL 14
POWER CONTROL

OBJECTIVE:
To develop body control and practice rebounding techniques and footwork.

DESCRIPTION:
The drill initially involves two players who assume a position in the foul circle. One player acts as a defensive player (O), while the other serves as the offensive player (X). The drill begins with both players facing each other. On a signal, (O) turns toward the basket, using an open pivot. (O) then attempts to force (X) out of the circle using (O)s rear end, hips, and arms. After a preset number of successful repetitions, the players interchange positions.

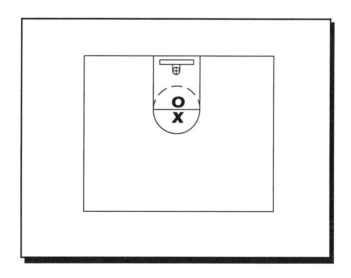

DRILL 15
RING AROUND THE ROSIE

OBJECTIVE:
To develop footwork and proper rebounding position.

DESCRIPTION:
The drill involves four players—two each on defense (X) and on offense (O). The primary focus of the drill is to get and maintain proper rebounding position. The drill begins by having (X) place (X)'s rear into the belly of (O). (O) attempts to duck inside of (X) by using an elbow to obtain a good rebounding position. If (O) goes too far under the basket, (O) should hook (X) and go back around to get an outside position and force (X) inside. The coach should stress to all of the participants to keep their elbows out and hands up and to use proper footwork.

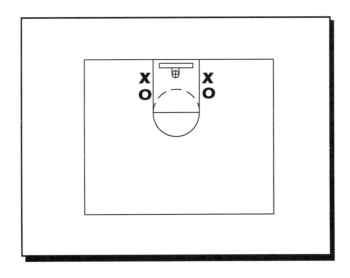

DRILL 16
TIPPING

OBJECTIVE:
To practice tipping skills and techniques.

DESCRIPTION:
The drill involves two players. The two players assume positions on opposite sides of the free throw lane, close to the backboard. The drill is initiated by having one player tip the ball to the other player, who in turn tips the ball back to that player (Diagram 1). The drill is continuous for a predetermined number of tips or a preset length of time. On the last tip, the player attempts to score. The players then rotate.

VARIATION:
*   All players continuously tip their own rebounds against the board (Diagram 2).

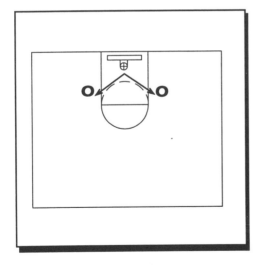

Diagram 1

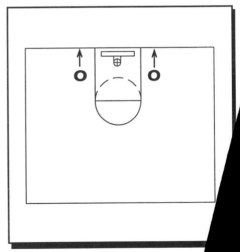

Diagram 2

DRILL 17
TIP OUT

OBJECTIVE:
To develop tipping skills and techniques.

DESCRIPTION:
The players are divided into two lines with each group facing the other at the free throw line. The drill begins by having the coach (C)—who is standing in the circle equidistant between the two groups—bounce the ball off the floor as hard as possible so that it goes as high into the air as possible. Once the ball hits the floor, the first player in each line steps to the ball and attempts to tip the ball back to the next player in the tipper's line. To the extent possible, the players should form up in line according to height. After each attempted tip, the players rotate. The drill continues for a predetermined number of successful tips or a set length of time.

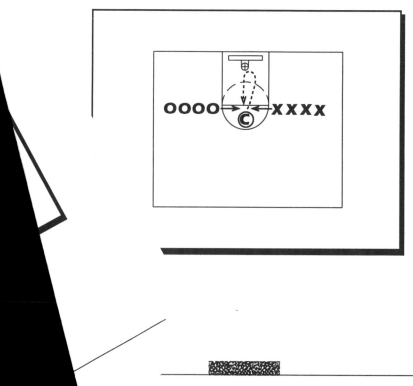

DRILL 18
ALLEY OOP AND OFF-THE-BOARD TIP UP

OBJECTIVE:
To practice tipping techniques after a rebounded shot.

DESCRIPTION:
The players form a single line. The first player in line serves as the rebounder (X). The drill begins by having the coach (C) throw an alley oop pass above and just to the left of the basket. (X) attempts to tip the ball into the basket. (C) then intentionally shoots a shot off the backboard which (X) again attempts to tip into the basket. After a predetermined number of attempted tips or successful tips, the players rotate. The rebounder goes to the end of the line and the next player becomes the new rebounder.

VARIATIONS:
- Players should work both sides of the basket.
- The squad should divide into several small groups and work at several baskets simultaneously.

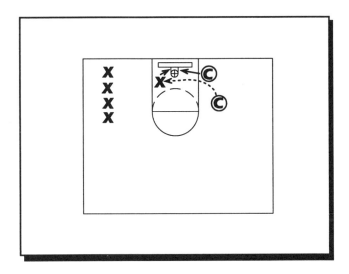

DRILL 19
TAKE CONTROL

OBJECTIVE:
To develop body control and to practice controlling techniques, footwork, and re-bounding skills.

DESCRIPTION:
The drill involves three players—two on offense (O) and one on defense (X). The players assume a position in front of and facing the basket, with (X) between the two (O)s. On command, (X) throws the basketball off the backboard and rebounds it— without any opposition from the two offensive players who are in front and be-hind (X). After retrieving the ball, (X)—using an open pivot and his body—takes the (O) behind him out. The (O) in front is simply controlled by (X).

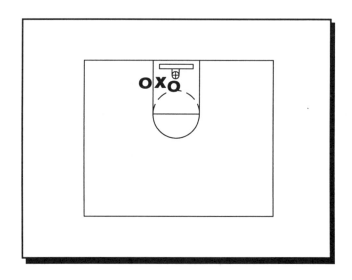

CHAPTER 2

CLEARING-OUT DRILLS

DRILL 20
INSIDE AND REVERSE PIVOT DRILL

OBJECTIVE:
To practice inside and reverse pivot moves for clearing out.

DESCRIPTION:
The players divide into two groups and pair-off and face the basket. One group is designated on offense (O) and one group on defense (X). The coach (C) points in the direction the offensive players should move after shooting an imaginary shot. The defensive players grab an imaginary rebound, practice inside and reverse pivot moves to clear out, and make an imaginary outlet pass. The drill is repeated for a predetermined number of repetitions.

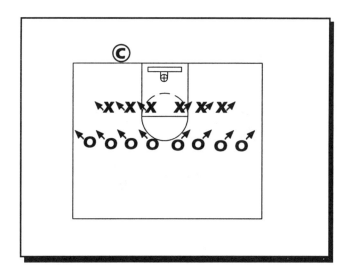

DRILL 21
SIX-SPOT DRILL

OBJECTIVE:
To practice clearing-out and getting into the proper position for rebounding.

DESCRIPTION:
The drill involves six players—three each designated as either offense (O) or defense (X). The drill is designed to be progressively more involved and demanding. Initially, the coach (C) blows a whistle, the (O)s remain stationary, and the (X)s block out in anticipation of going to the boards to get the rebound. Next, while no shot continues to be taken, the (O)s move any way/direction they want on the sound of the whistle. The (X)s must clear them out again. The final step is to have the coach shoot the ball and have the players perform the aforementioned actions while going for a live rebound. After a predetermined number of repetitions, the (X)s rotate to offense and the (O)s become defensive players.

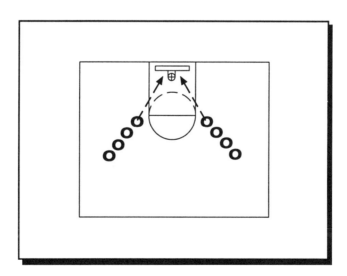

DRILL 22
ONE-ON-ONE IN THE LANE

OBJECTIVE:
To develop clearing-out skills, footwork, and defensive techniques.

DESCRIPTION:
The drill involves two players (P-1 and P-X) a coach (C), and a basketball. The team forms a line at mid-court. The first two players assume a position in front of the mid-court line in an extension of the foul lane. P-1 is on offense, while P-X is the defender. During the drill, P-X's hands must remain locked behind P-X's back. The focus is to make P-X use his feet and head. The drill begins with P-1 with the ball. P-1 is attempting to score under restricted conditions. P-1 is limited to two dribbles. P-1 can pass to the (C) and try to get open to receive a pass back. P-X attempts to deny P-1 open access to shoot and access to receive a return pass from (C). When P-1 shoots, P-X must box out P-1 to deny P-1 access to the rebound. If the missed shot hits the floor, the drill is over and players rotate. If P-1 gets the rebound before the ball hits the floor, P-X remains on defense.

COACHING POINTS:
- P-1 must remain in the extended foul lane during the drill.
- P-1 can be restricted by using only certain moves (e.g., crossover moves, reverse moves, etc.).

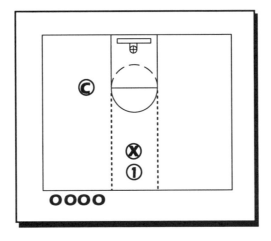

DRILL 23
FAKE OUT, CLEAR OUT

OBJECTIVE:
To practice clearing-out techniques and teach faking techniques, defensive concentration.

DESCRIPTION:
The drill involves having the players form into two lines—one on the baseline and one above the free throw circle. The baseline players are on defense, while the on-court players have an offensive role. The first player in each line assumes a position facing each other on the free throw line. The back of the defender (O) is turned toward the coach (C) who is positioned under the basket. The drill commences by having the coach roll a basketball toward one of three predetermined spots under the basket. The offensive player (X) is then required to fake out (O), run, pick up the ball, and shoot it. (O) attempts to clear out (X), using a shuffle step and reverse pivot. (O) then runs to the ball, picks it up, and hands it to the (C). All players are encouraged to move their feet quickly and stay on their feet. The drill continues for a preset period of time.

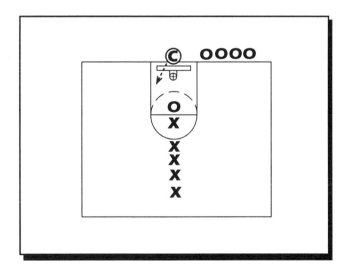

DRILL 24
SHOT AFTER PASS

OBJECTIVE:
To practice rebounding and clearing-out techniques.

DESCRIPTION:
The players form up into a single line facing the basket. The drill involves two players—a defensive player (X) and an offensive player (O). The drill begins when (X) who has the basketball passes it to (O)—the first player in line. (X) follows the pass and then strongly defends against (O). (O) either drives to the basket and attempts to score or shoots the ball immediately after receiving the pass if (X) is in poor defensive position. If (O) misses the shot, both (X) and (O) go for the rebound. (X) attempts to clear out (O) before going for the rebound. If (O) makes the shot, (X) goes to the end of the line and the next player in line becomes the new defender.

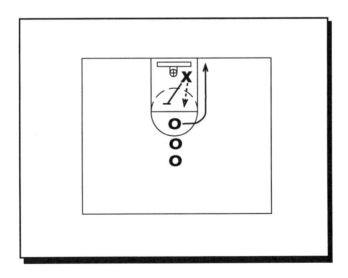

DRILL 25
REBOUNDING FROM THE "HOLE"

OBJECTIVE:
To practice rebounding and clearing-out techniques.

DESCRIPTION:
The players form a single line along the sideline. The drill involves two players at a time—a defensive player (X) and an offensive player (O). The drill begins by having (O) dribble to the free throw line and shoot. (X) does not interfere with the shot. After the shot is in the air, (X) attempts to prevent (O) from rebounding the ball. (X), disregarding the ball initially, focuses attention on the shooter for two full counts before sealing off and going for the rebound. Players receive a point for either making a shot or getting a rebound. The drill continues until a player scores a preset number of points.

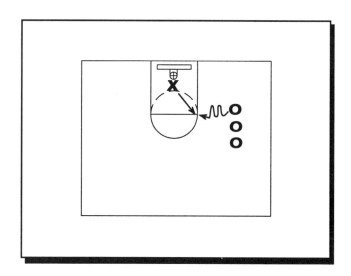

DRILL 26
BLOCKING OUT THE SHOOTER

OBJECTIVE:
To practice rebounding and clearing-out techniques.

DESCRIPTION:
The players form two lines—one positioned at the free throw line facing the basket and one underneath the basket facing the other line. The players underneath the basket are on defense, while the players at the free throw line are on offense. The first player in each line participates in the drill. The drill begins by having (O), who has a basketball, pass the ball to (X). As soon as the pass is made, (O) quickly charges out to defend (X) by getting a hand in (O)'s face, yelling at (O), and blocking (O) out after (O) shoots. Upon receiving the pass, (O) immediately shoots a jump shot. (O) does not wait for (X) to get into the proper defensive position. Once (O) has shot the ball, both (O) and (X) go for the rebound. (X) attempts to clear out (O). If (O) makes the shot or (X) gets a rebound, the drill ends. Each player goes to the end of the opposite line and the next two players become the new participants in the drill.

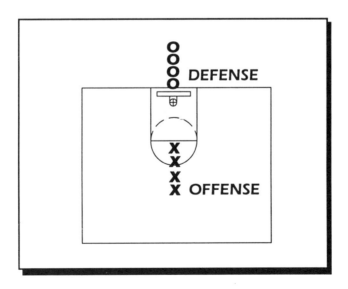

DRILL 27
TWO-PLAYER BOX-OUT SWITCH

OBJECTIVE:
To practice clearing-out techniques and to develop footwork.

DESCRIPTION:
The drill involves four players—two on defense (X) and two on offense (O). The two (O)s stand behind the foul line, slightly outside the foul lane area. The two (X)s assume a position outside the foul lane area, approximately six feet closer to the basket than the (O)s. The drill begins by having the coach (C) take a shot. As soon as the shot is released, the (O)s attempt to crash the boards to get an offensive rebound. The (X)s clear out the opposite (O)s. The (X)s then crash the boards to get the rebound. If the (X)s get the rebound, the players switch roles. If the (O)s get the rebound, the drill is repeated with the players in the same roles.

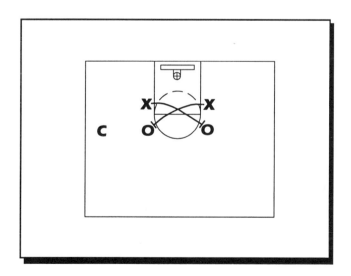

DRILL 28
THREE-ON-THREE-ON-THREE

OBJECTIVE:
To practice clearing-out and rebounding techniques.

DESCRIPTION:
The players form into three lines. The first player in each line is designated as a defensive player (X), while the other players serve as offensive players (O). The drill begins by having the player with the ball (O-3) shoot. The three offensive players (O-1, O-2, O-3) then go for an offensive rebound, while the three defenders (X-1, X-2, X-3) clear out. If the (X)s get the rebound, they pass the ball to the next group of players in line (O-4, O-5, O-6). The first group of (O)s then become the defensive group. If the (O)s get the rebound, they shoot it again. If any shot is made and the offense can grab the ball, the (O)s shoot again. Only when the (X)s get possession of the ball does play stop and the players rotate roles. A scoring system awarding one point for a made shot or a defensive rebound can be used. The first group to earn a preset number of points wins.

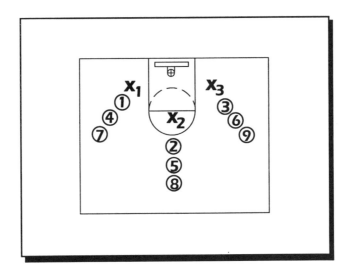

DRILL 29
THREE-ON-THREE SIMULATED REBOUND

OBJECTIVE:
To practice rebounding and clearing-out techniques.

DESCRIPTION:
The drill involves six players—three on offense (0-1, 0-2, 0-3) and three on defense (X-1, X-2, X-3). O1, O2 and O3 assume a variety of positions to simulate rebounding in a variety of common offensive and defensive placements (triangle, wing, point, corner, high post, and low post). On a signal, all players simulate going for a rebound. The defensive players clear out the offensive players before going for the imaginary rebound.

VARIATION:
• The coach can throw the ball off the backboard and have all six players go for an actual rebound.

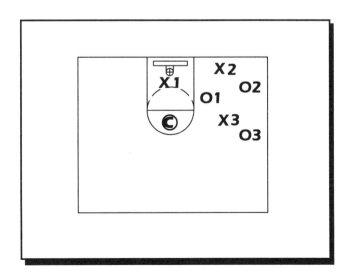

DRILL 30
MORE THREE-ON-THREE SIMULATED REBOUNDING

OBJECTIVE:
To practice rebounding, clearing-out, and movement patterns.

DESCRIPTION:
The drill involves six players—three on offense (O-1, O-2, O-3) and three on defense (X-1, X-2, X-3). The six players, while attempting to get a simulated rebound, are assigned specific tasks or movement patterns. On a signal, O-1 goes to the outside, O-2 goes to the imaginary ball, and O-3 goes to the free throw line. On defense, X-1 quickly attempts to jam O-1 and reads the movement of the offensive players; X-2 clears out (O-2) and continues to focus on preventing O-2 from getting to the basket; and X-3 anticipates a long rebound coming to the free throw line.

VARIATION:
• A coach can toss a ball off the backboard and have a live "rebound" situation.

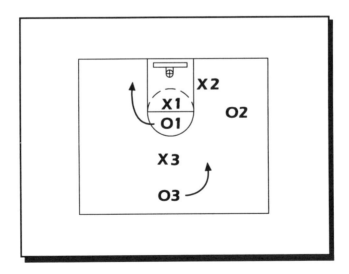

DRILL 31
EVEN MORE THREE-ON-THREE SIMULATED REBOUNDING

OBJECTIVE:
To practice rebounding, clearing-out techniques, and movement patterns.

DESCRIPTION:
The drill involves six players—three on offense (O-1, O-2, O-3) and on defense (X-1, X-2, X-3). The six players, while attempting to get a simulated rebound, are assigned specific tasks or movement patterns. On a signal, (O-1) goes to the empty area under the basket, O-2 goes to the middle of the lane, and O-3 goes to the free throw lane area. On defense, X-1 forces O-1 to the outside; X-2 cuts off O-2's access to the basket and seals off high; and X-3 mirrors O-3 and protects the free throw area.

VARIATION:
•   A coach can toss a ball off the backboard and have a "live" rebound situation.

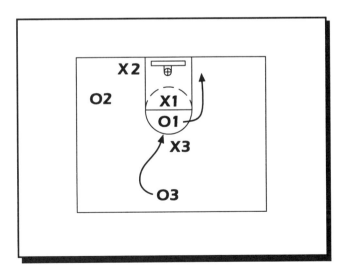

DRILL 32
FIVE-ON-FIVE CLEAR OUT

OBJECTIVE:
To practice clearing-out and basic rebounding techniques.

DESCRIPTION:
The drill involves ten players engaged in five-on-five competition. One group of players is on offense (O), while the other is on defense (X). The drill is initiated by having the coach (C) throw the ball off the rim. All players aggressively go for the rebound. The (X)s create contact with the (O)s by pivoting into the (O)s, bending back, and legally using their elbows. The (X)s hold their contact, then step forward, and jump.

COACHING POINT:
*   The (X)s should concentrate on pivoting into the (O)s when clearing-out.

VARIATIONS:
*   The (O)s can be required to run a five-to-ten-pass weave before the coach shoots.
*   The (C) can also pass to one of the open (O)s who would then shoot it immediately.

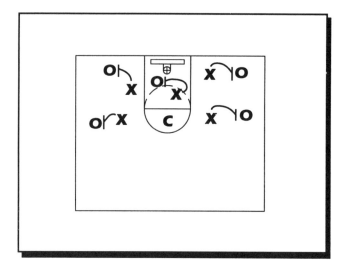

DRILL 33
CROSS CLEARING-OUT ON A FREE THROW

OBJECTIVE:
To practice cross clearing-out techniques in a free throw situation.

DESCRIPTION:
The drill is designed to have members of the shooting team (O-1 to O-5) in a free throw situation use cross clearing-out techniques in an attempt to gain a positional advantage over the defensive team (X-1 to X-5) after the free throw has left the shooter's hand. As the shot is being attempted, O-5 crosses the lane and tries to get a rebound position inside of X-4. Simultaneously, O-4 crosses behind O-5 and attempts to get an inside position under the basket. In a game situation, the use of the cross clearing-out technique is frequently initiated on a signal from the coach.

COACHING POINT:
• If a squad has 15 players, the drill can be conducted with three teams of five players each.

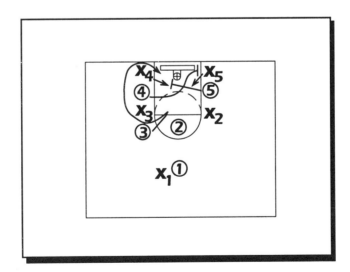

CHAPTER 3

BLOCKING-OUT DRILLS

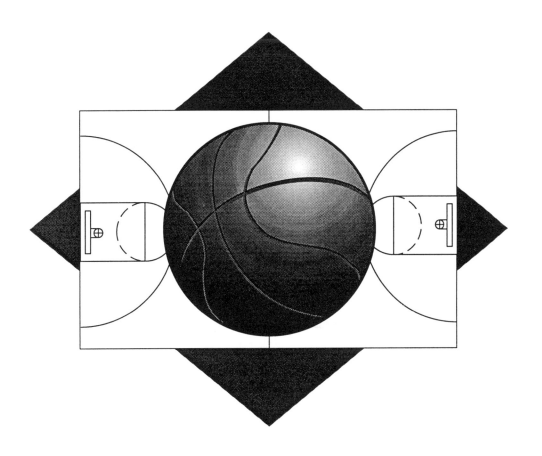

DRILL 34
BLOCK THE SHOOTER

OBJECTIVE:
To practice blocking out, outlet passing, and rebounding techniques.

DESCRIPTION:
The drill involves three players and a coach. One player (D) assumes a defensive position on the free throw line. (D) is flanked by two players on offense (O). The coach (C) stands in front of the three players and passes the ball to an offensive player. (D) immediately moves to defend against (O) who shoots the ball. (D) blocks out (O), secures the rebound, and makes an outlet pass back to (C). (D) and (O) interchange positions, and the drill continues.

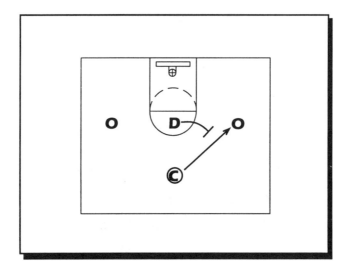

DRILL 35
ONE-ON-ONE BLOCK OUT

OBJECTIVE:
To develop ball-handling skills, teach blocking out and outlet passing, and practice rebounding techniques.

DESCRIPTION:
The drill involves three players. X-3 has the ball and goes one-on-one against X-1 and attempts to score. If the shot is made, X-1 treats it as a rebound and outlets a pass to X-2. If the shot is missed, X-1 blocks out X-3 and gets the rebound. X-2 goes to the side of the court where the rebound is retrieved by X-1 and calls for the ball. X-1 then passes the ball to X-2 who drives the middle of the lane. X-1 goes behind X-2 and fills the lane. X-2 shoots a lay-up on the opposite side from where X-3 originally started. X-1 reacts according to whether the shot is made or missed. If X-3 scores in the initial one-on-one competition, X-3 continues to participate in the drill. Otherwise, all players rotate to new positions.

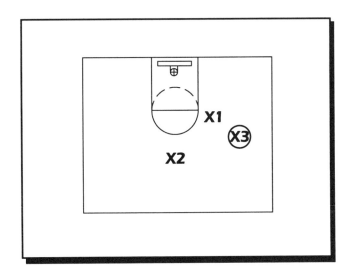

DRILL 36
PRESSURE BOX-OUT

OBJECTIVE:
To practice blocking-out techniques.

DESCRIPTION:
The drill involves having two players (X) and (O) assume a back-to-back position in the middle of the foul line. Both players stand upright. On the coach's whistle, both players immediately assume a proper box-out position—feet in a wide base, legs bent, and arms and elbows up and locked—and make contact with their buttocks. Staying on the balls of their feet, (X) and (O) exert pressure against each other and try to force one another out of the foul circle. At all times during the drill, (X) and (O) should maintain contact in a back-to-back (butt-to-butt) position.

COACHING POINTS:
- The coach should emphasize to the players that they should work on establishing a strong, sturdy, clear-out position.
- The coach should emphasize to the players that boxing-out does not require moving their opponents backwards ten feet or more.

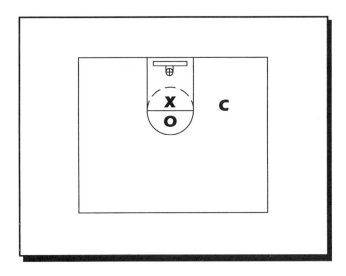

DRILL 37
THE DUMMY REBOUND

OBJECTIVE:
To practice footwork, blocking out, and outlet passing.

DESCRIPTION:
The drill involves three players—two defenders (X-1 and X-2) and an offensive player (O). One defender and (O) go one-on-one against each other without the ball. The coach (C) throws the ball off the backboard to the side where the pair of competing players is positioned (approximately 8-10 feet from the basket). (O) offers controlled, simulated movements to the basket, which forces X-1 to use proper footwork to box-out (O) while going for the rebound. X-2 concentrates on controlling the ball and making a good outlet pass to X-2 who has assumed a position along the nearest sideline. X-1 is encouraged to get the rebound before it hits the floor.

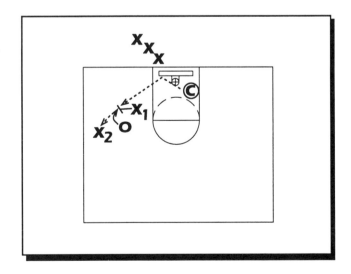

DRILL 38
TWO-ON-TWO BLOCK OUT

OBJECTIVE:
To practice rebounding and blocking-out techniques.

DESCRIPTION:
The drill involves four players—two on offense (O-1 and O-2) and two on defense (X-1 and X-2). The drill begins by having the coach (C) shoot the ball. Once the shot is taken, X-1 and X-2 use one of the various methods for blocking out and then go for the rebound. If one of the defenders gets the rebound, the drill ends and the players switch roles. If the offensive players get the rebound, all players remain in their roles and the drill is repeated.

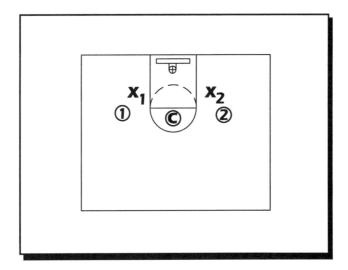

DRILL 39
THREE-ON-THREE,
BLOCKING OUT THE SHOOTER

OBJECTIVE:
To practice blocking-out and rebounding techniques.

DESCRIPTION:
The drill involves competing three-player groups. The drill is initiated with three pairs of players facing each other—one pair at the top of the circle and one pair on each wing. One member of each pair is on defense (O), while the other player is on offense (X). The coach (C) shoots the ball to begin the drill. All six players aggressively go for the rebound. The (O)s attempt to block out the (X)s before going for the ball. The players switch positions after a preset number of shots.

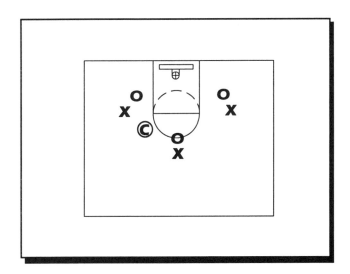

DRILL 40
THREE-ON-THREE BLOCKING-OUT CONTEST

OBJECTIVE:
To practice defensive positioning, boxing-out, and rebounding techniques; to have offensive players work on avoiding being blocked out and going hard to the offensive boards.

DESCRIPTION:
The drill is designed primarily for front court players. It involves six players—three on offense (F, F, C) and three on defense (X, X, X). The two forwards (F, F) initially assume positions on the wing, while the center (C) takes a low-post position. The drill begins by having a coach (CO) and a manager (MA), who are located in the front court area, pass the ball back and forth until one decides to shoot. As the ball is passed out front, the (X)s make the proper defensive slides. Once the ball is shot, both the (X)s and the offensive players go for the rebound. The (X)s block out, while the offensive players attempt to circumvent the block. Regardless of which group gets the rebound, the ball is passed back out to the (CO) and the drill continues for a preset number of repetitions.

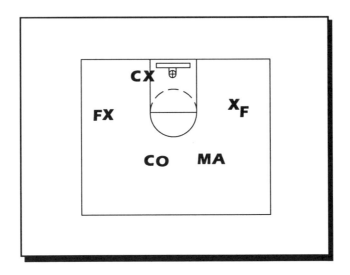

DRILL 41
TWO-LINE REBOUNDING

OBJECTIVE:
To teach boxing out and the techniques of aggressive rebounding; to develop the ability to make outlet passes; to improve offensive rebounding skills.

DESCRIPTION:
The players form two lines facing the basket, one at each end of the free throw line. The first player in each line acts as a defensive player (X), while all of the other players serve offensive (O) roles. The drill begins by having the coach (C) shoot the ball. The two (X)s then box out the first player in each line (O). The two (O)s crash the board, while the (X)s attempt to hold them out, rebound the missed shot, and throw an outlet pass to a manager (M) positioned in the outlet area. The two offensive players then go to the end of the line and are replaced by the next man in each line. The drill continues with the same (X)s against all of the (O)s—two at a time. Once the (X)s have defended against all of the offensive players, they go to the end of the offensive player line and two new defenders take their place.

COACHING POINTS:
- The lines to practice rebounding from different areas and positions can be moved.
- A reasonable amount of physical contact can be permitted.
- A scoring system that rewards the defenders who get the most rebounds can be used.
- The (C) and (M) a variety of options: (1) shoot immediately; (2) pass to each other and then shoot; or (3) pass to one of the (O)s who then shoots can be given.

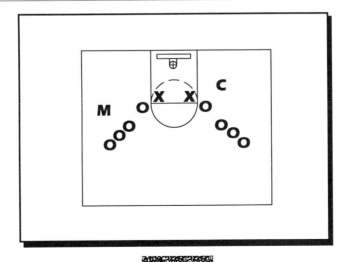

DRILL 42
BASELINE BOX-OUT

OBJECTIVE:
To practice boxing-out and rebounding techniques.

DESCRIPTION:
The drill involves six players—three on offense (O) and three on defense (X). The drill begins by having the coach (C) shoot the ball. Once the shot is taken, the (X)s immediately box out and then aggressively go to the boards. Both the (X)s and the (O)s attempt to get the rebound. The competitive aspects of the drill can be enhanced by establishing goals for the (X)s and (O)s. For example, the (X)s can be required to get three rebounds in three shots, while the (O)s can be required to rebound at least one of three shots. Failure by either group to achieve its goal can result in punitive action (e.g., run sprints, do five-finger push-ups, jump for imaginary rebounds, etc.). Both groups should be required to closely adhere to using proper rebounding techniques.

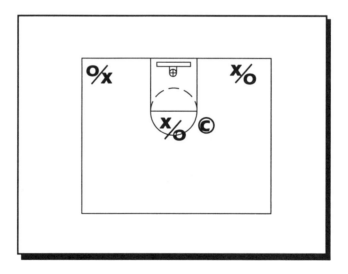

CHAPTER 4

OUTLET PASSING DRILLS

DRILL 43
IMAGINARY REBOUNDING

OBJECTIVE:
Develop the techniques for outlet passing and practice rebounding movement patterns.

DESCRIPTION:
All players spread out facing the coach who assumes a position in front of the basket. On command, the coach throws the ball up at the basket. Imagining that they are in position to rebound the ball, the players practice the proper techniques of both rebounding the ball as it comes off the backboard and then throwing an outlet pass. The coach designates which pivot to use to clear out and which side to throw an imaginary pass.

VARIATIONS:
*   Half of the players could be designated as defensive players and half as offensive players. On the shot, the defenders can practice clearing out offensive players while the offensive players go to the board for an imaginary rebound.
*   On the coach's command, the players can advance from performing the drill at half-speed to full speed.

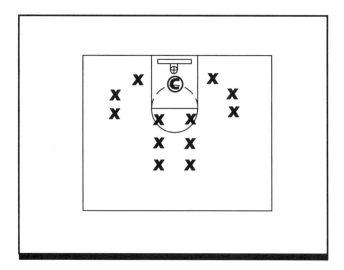

DRILL 44
REBOUND AND RELEASE

OBJECTIVE:
To practice outlet passing and rebounding techniques.

DESCRIPTION:
The drill involves two players (X-1 and X-2). X-1 shoots the ball from the free throw line. X-2 stands in the middle of the lane and rebounds the shot if it misses. If the shot is made, X-1 shoots again. After shooting the ball, X-1 goes to the wing area on the side of the basket on which the ball bounds and awaits an outlet pass from X-2. X-2 rebounds the ball using proper form and outlets to X-1. The drill is conducted for a preset length of time, and then the players switch roles. While the drill is live, all players are encouraged to give a maximum effort.

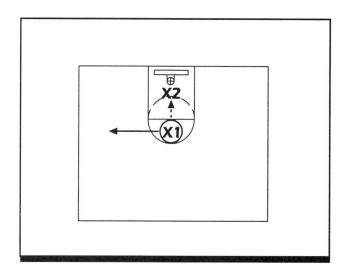

DRILL 45
OUTLET PASSING

OBJECTIVE:
To practice rebounding techniques and develop outlet passing skills.

DESCRIPTION:
The players form a single line facing the basket. One player assumes a position to receive an outlet pass above the five-second hash mark. The drill is initiated by having the first player in line throw the ball up high on the backborad. That player then attempts to rebound the ball at its maximum height. After rebounding the ball, the player turns to the outside and makes an outlet pass using either a baseball pass or a two-hand, over-the-head pass to the outlet player. The outlet player then throws the ball to the next player in the front of the line. The outlet player goes to the end of the line, while the rebounder becomes the outlet player. The drill is run in a quick, continous manner for a predetermined number of repetitions or length of time.

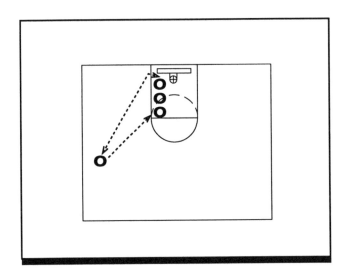

DRILL 46
TWO-LINE REBOUNDING WITH AN OUTLET PASS

OBJECTIVE:
To practice rebounding and outlet pass techniques.

DESCRIPTION:
The squad is divided into two equal-sized groups, each of which lines up on one end of the free throw line facing the basket. The first player in each line (P-1 and P-7) assumes a position on the adjacent wing. The first two players remaining in each line (P-2, P-3, P-8 and P-9) have a ball. The drill procedures are identical for each line and include the following steps: P-2 throws the ball up on the backboard and rebounds the ball using proper techniques. P-1 steps away and then cuts back toward the basket to receive an outlet pass from P-2. After receiving the outlet pass, P-1 passes the ball to the next person in line who does not have a ball (P-4). P-1 then goes to the end of the opposite line. P-3—who already had a ball—then throws the ball up on the backboard, rebounds the ball, and outlets to P-2, who after passing to P-1, has sprinted out to the wing (P-1's old position) and has cut back to receive the pass. The drill involves ongoing action. The steps are continuously repeated. Two balls are in play for each group.

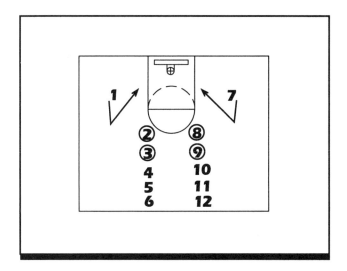

DRILL 47
ONE-ON-ONE WITH AN OUTLET PASS

OBJECTIVE:
To practice both offensive and defensive rebounding techniques; to improve outlet passing skills.

DESCRIPTION:
The coach sets up at the free throw line, while the players line up in a single file facing the basket. The first player in line (P-1) assumes a defensive position (to guard P-3). The second player in line (P-2) takes a position on the wing. The player remaining first in line (P-3) prepares to battle for the rebound against P-1. The drill commences by having the coach shoot the ball. P-3 goes for an offensive rebound, while P-1 clears out and attempts to get a defensive rebound. Whoever gets the rebound throws an outlet pass to P-2, who has taken a step away and then comes back to receive the pass. If P-1 has rebounded the shot, P-2 then passes the ball to the coach, and the players rotate—P-3 to P-1's position, P-1 to P-2, and P-2 to the back of the line. If, however, P-3 gets the offensive rebound, P-3 rotates to P-2's position, P-2 goes to the back of the line, while P-1 remains in place as the defensive rebounder.

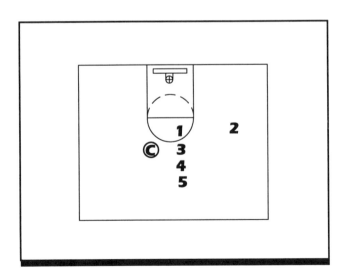

DRILL 48
REBOUND-PASS OUT

OBJECTIVE:
To practice rebounding skills and outlet passing.

DESCRIPTION:
A player is placed at each wing position (P-2 and P-3) and a line of players assume a position out front at the top of the key (P-1, P-4, P-5). The first player in line (P-1) passes to either wing who is moving to receive the pass. After passing the ball, P-1 cuts to the basket and receives a return pass from the wing with the ball. P-1 then throws the ball off the board, rebounds the ball, and makes a strong outlet pass back to the wing who originally had passed the ball to P-1. That wing then tosses the ball back to the next player in line (P-4) and goes to the end of the line. P-1 then replaces the vacated wing, and the process is repeated.

COACHING POINTS:

- The cutter going to the basket should go away from the wing who received the first pass and then make a good, hard cut to the basket.
- The drill can involve from 4-12 players.
- All players should be required to hustle continuously.

VARIATION:
- The coach can specify whether the wing should make a bounce pass or a chest pass to the cutter.

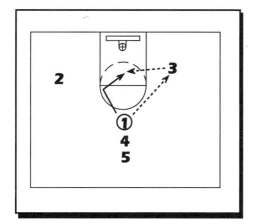 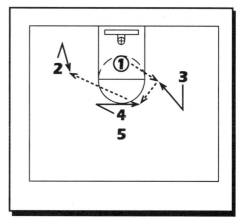

DRILL 49
REBOUND AND OUTLET

OBJECTIVE:
To practice outlet passes, transitional moves, and rebounding skills.

DESCRIPTION:
The players form a single line and form up near the side line. The first player in line is designated as the rebounder and assumes a position in the point. The drill begins by having the coach (C) toss the ball on the backboard. The rebounder recovers (rebounds) the ball and throws an outlet pass to the next player in line who is breaking to mid-court. The rebounder then immediately follows up the pass and backs up the receiver who—after receiving the pass—has dribbled to the other basket for a lay-up. The rebounder and the receiver go to the end of the line. The players rotate positions. The drill continues until each player has participated a predetermined number of times both as a rebounder and as a receiver. The emphasis should focus on having the rebounder make a quick outlet pass and smooth transition.

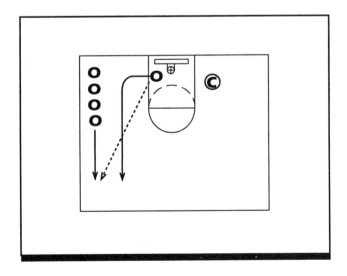

DRILL 50
SLIDE, BLOCK, AND GO

OBJECTIVE:
To practice applying defensive pressure, defensive rebounding techniques, and outlet passing.

DESCRIPTION:
The drill involves three players—one defensive and two offensive, a coach, and one basketball. The coach assumes a position across the foul line. The defensive player (X) assumes a zone position just beyond the foul circle with feet placed wide and moving and hands up in the passing lanes. The offensive players (O) take flanking positions, adjacent to (X). The coach passes the ball to either offensive player, forcing (X) to move to the ball. The ball should be passed just beyond (X)'s reach. Once (O) has received the pass, (O) then shoots a jump shot just over the extended defensive reach of (X). A shot rim is used to force a rebound. Once the shot is in the air, (X) goes to the ball, rebounds the ball, quickly outlets a pass to the coach, and gets ready to go again.

COACHING POINT:
•   (X) should be instructed to attempt to block (O)'s shot by jumping straight up—as opposed to at (O).

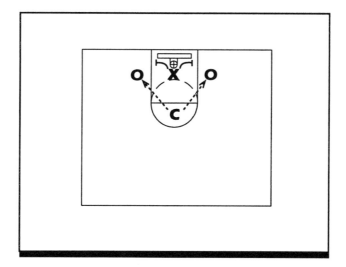

DRILL 51
CHECK THE REBOUNDER

OBJECTIVE:
To practice rebounding techniques and develop the skills involved in outlet passing against pressure.

DESCRIPTION:
The drill involves three players. The drill is initiated by having P-1 throw the ball against the backboard, go to the ball, and strongly rebound it. At that point, P-2 applies defensive pressure against P-1. P-1 fakes, clears, and makes a sharp outlet pass to P-3.

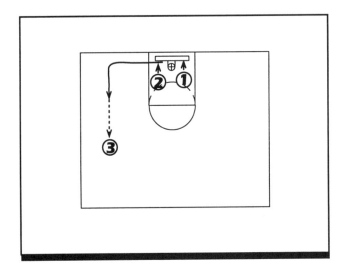

DRILL 52
AGAINST THE TRIO

OBJECTIVE:
To teach defenders to clear out the defensive boards, get the rebound, and throw an accurate outlet pass.

DESCRIPTION:
The drill involves four players. The drill begins by having the coach (C) pass the ball to an offensive player (P-1), who then goes one-on-one against a defender (X-1). P-1 drives on X-1. X-1 attempts to keep P-1 under control. Once P-1 shoots, X-1 blocks P-1 off the boards. If the shot is made, X-1 throws the ball to either P-2 or P-3. If the shot is missed, X-1 outlet passes the rebound (before X-1 hits the floor) to either P-2 or P-3. The difficulty of the drill can be increased by having P-1 attempt to steal the pass from either P-2 or P-3. After X-1 passes, the player not receiving the pass flash pivots. X-1 attempts to drag the flash pivot. Once the new player receives the pass, X-1 goes one-on-one against that player. Subsequently, that player shoots, X-1 rebounds, and passes to the third player. Should the shot be made, the shooter attempts to steal the pass from the third player. After X-1 has played defense against all three, the players rotate roles.

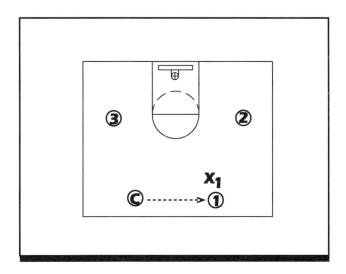

DRILL 53
DRIVE IT

OBJECTIVE:
To practice rebounding techniques, outlet passing, dribbling skills, and playing one-on-one offense and defense.

DESCRIPTION:
The players are divided into three groups (designated as A, B, and C). Group B members serve as the rebounders who make the outlet pass. Group A players receive the outlet pass and drive straight to the opposite basket. Members of Group C act as the defenders. One member of each group participates in the drill at any one time. The drill begins by having Player B throw the ball off the backboard, rebound it, and throw an outlet pass to Player A who then drives for a lay-up. Once Player A gets the ball, Player C—who starts near the hash mark—sprints down the court and attempts to turn the dribbler (Player A). Players A and C then play one-on-one until either the offense scores or Player C rebounds or steals the ball. After each series, the players rotate positions clockwise.

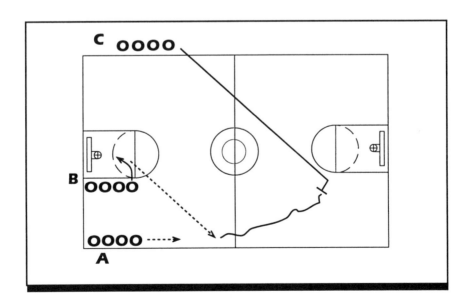

DRILL 54
FOUR-PERSON DELAY

OBJECTIVE:
To practice outlet passing, movement skills, and rebounding techniques.

DESCRIPTION:
The drill involves four players—two rebounders and two outlet (wing) players. The drill begins by having the rebounder with a ball throw it against the backboard. The other rebounder leaps high, gets the rebound, and throws a pass to the nearest outlet player. The outlet player who receives the ball then passes it to the other wing player who is cutting to the middle of the court (referred to as the "middle player"). The middle player dribbles the ball up the court and then passes it back to the outlet player, who is trailing the play. The rebounder who originally started the drill by throwing the ball off the board, fills the weak side lane and crosses the three-second area. The outlet player with the ball then selects among several scoring options.

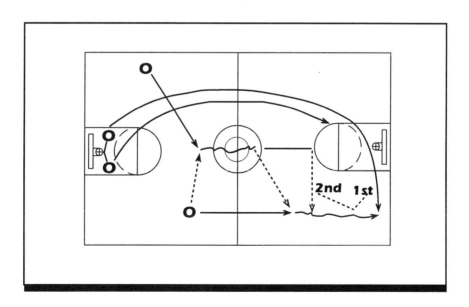

CHAPTER 5

FAST-BREAK DRILLS

DRILL 55
THREE-ON-THREE GO FOR IT

OBJECTIVE:
To practice rebounding, clearing out, and fast-break transition techniques.

DESCRIPTION:
The drill involves six players—three each on offense (O) and defense (X). The drill begins when the coach (C) shoots the ball. All six players attack the board in an attempt to get the rebound. The (X)s clear out the (O)s. If the (X)s get the rebound, they fast break to the other basket and try to score. If the (O)s gets the rebound, they shoot the ball as soon as they have a shot. Score is kept. The first team to score a preset number of points wins.

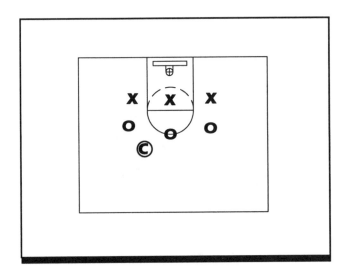

DRILL 56
REBOUND-AND-BREAK

OBJECTIVE:
To practice offensive and defensive rebounding techniques, clearing-out skills, and outlet passing for the break.

DESCRIPTION:
The drill involves two five-player teams—one team each on offense (O) and defense (X). The (O)s assume a position initially outside the foul lane, while the (X)s engage in a player-to-player defense. The drill begins by having the coach (C) take a shot. On the shot, both teams aggressively go for the rebound. The (X)s attempt to clear out the (O)s before getting the defensive rebound. The (O)s attempt to work through the blocks to get an offensive rebound. If the (X)s get the ball, they attempt to run a fast break and score. At the same time, the (O)s convert to defense. If the (X)s don't get a quick score, they then run the team's secondary fast-break offense against a player-to-player defense used by the (O)s. The team that rebounds and runs a fast-break continues in that role until one of two things happen: either they don't score or the original offensive team gets an offensive rebound. After each fast break—whether a basket is made or not—the ball is returned to the coach who resets the players and shoots to start the drill again.

VARIATION:
• The coach can vary the drill by shooting from different positions on the floor.

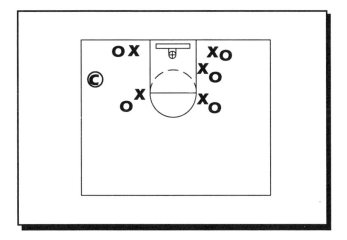

DRILL 57
OUTLET AND BREAK

OBJECTIVE:
To practice rebounding techniques and outlet passing skills.

DESCRIPTION:
The players form up into four lines—two along the outside of the foul lane and two on the opposite wings. The drill begins by having the coach (C) shoot the ball which is then rebounded by the first two players in the foul lane lines—X-1 and X-6. Depending on which player gets the rebound, the ball is outletted to either X-14 or X-11 on the wind. At that point, whichever player doesn't receive the outlet pass (either X-14 or X-11) breaks to the middle to get a pass from the player with the ball. Whichever player of the two original possible rebounders (X-1 or X-6) who didn't get the ball then breaks down the outside lane, receives a pass from the player currently with the basketball, and drives for a lay-up.

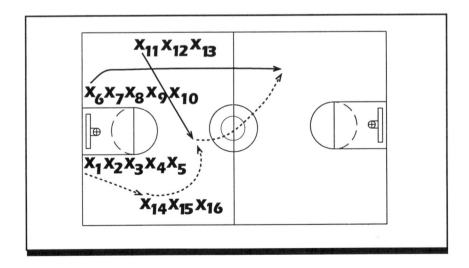

DRILL 58
THREE-MAN BOUND AND BREAK

OBJECTIVE:
To practice rebounding techniques, outlet passing, footwork, and fast-break movement patterns.

DESCRIPTION:
The drill involves three rebounders and two wing players. The drill begins by having the coach shoot from the free throw line. P-1, P-2, and P-3 aggressively go for the rebound. Whoever gets the rebound outlets a pass to the open wing player (P-4 or P-6). While waiting for the outlet pass, P-4 and P-6 execute multiple moves to get open. P-5 and P-7 defend against the outlet pass. Upon retrieving the ball, the rebounder has three primary options:

- Pass to the open wing on the rebounder's side of the court.
- Pass to the opposite wing, who is cutting to the middle of the court.
- Dribble the ball out and then pass to an open wing.

After making an outlet pass, the rebounder goes on a fast break with the two wing players (P-4 and P-6). Together they work to get the ball out of the backcourt. All other players wait to rotate into the drill.

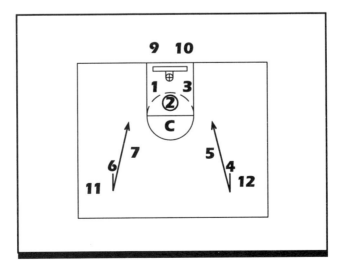

DRILL 59
TWO-MAN MIDDLE-MAN DRIBBLE
AND PASS

OBJECTIVE:
To practice dribbling, passing, and rebounding off the fast-break.

DESCRIPTION:
The players form two lines—one in the free throw lane and one on the wing. The first player in each line participates in the drill initially. The first player in the free throw lane line dribbles most of the length of the court, stops short of the top of the circle, and bounce passes it to the wing player who is cutting to the basket. The wing player shoots a lay-up, while the passing player rebounds the shot if it is missed.

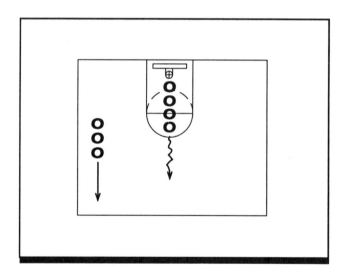

DRILL 60
REBOUND OUTLET

OBJECTIVE:
To practice outlet passing, filling the lanes on the fast break, and rebounding techniques.

DESCRIPTION:
The players form two lines—one each in the middle of the foul lane and on the wing. The first player in each line participates in the drill initially. The drill begins by having the rebounder (the first player in the foul lane line) throw the ball against the backboard, rebound it, and quickly make an outlet pass to the wing player (the first player in the wing line). The alternate outlet player (the second member of the wing line) then breaks to the center of the court and receives a pass from the outlet player. This player then drives to the basket, while the outlet player and the rebounder fill the lanes.

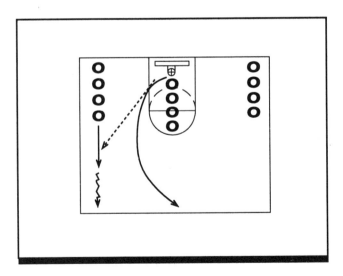

DRILL 61
GO-FOR-IT REBOUND

OBJECTIVE:
To practice rebounding techniques, outlet passing, and fast-break movement patterns.

DESCRIPTION:
The players form four lines. Two of the lines flank the outside of the free throw lane, while the other two are positioned on the wings. The drill begins by having the coach (C) shoot a free throw. The first player in each of the two middle lines (X-1 and X-6) aggressively goes for the rebound. Whoever gets the rebound outlets a pass to the nearest wing player (the first player in the two wing lines participates in the drill), either X-11 or X-14. The wing player, who does not receive the initial pass, then breaks to the middle of the court to receive a pass from the wing player with the ball. Simultaneously, the rebounder who did not get the rebound that started the drill breaks down the outside lane, receives a pass from the wing player with the ball, and drives to shoot a lay-up.

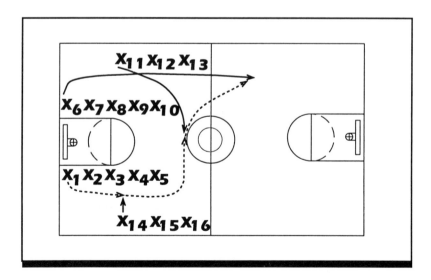

DRILL 62
QUICK REBOUND AND QUICK TRANSITION

OBJECTIVE:
To practice rebounding techniques, outlet passing, and movement patterns on the fast break; to develop stamina.

DESCRIPTION:
The drill involves two players—a rebounder (R) and an outlet player (O). The players who are not actively participating in the drill form a line behind the outlet player on the wing. The drill begins by having the coach (C) toss the ball off the backboard. (R) gets the ball and throws an outlet pass to (O) who is breaking toward mid-court. (R) immediately follows up the pass to (O) and backs up (O) who is driving to the other basket to shoot a lay-up. After (O) shoots a lay-out, the players rotate. The next two players in line become the (R) and (O), respectively. (R) should be encouraged to make a quick outlet pass and a quick transition during the skills.

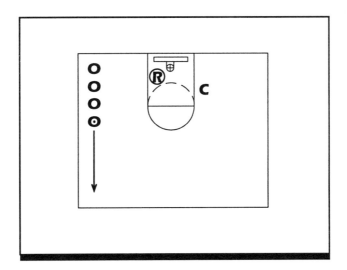

CHAPTER 6

ZONE DEFENSE DRILLS

DRILL 63
ZONE DEFENSE REBOUNDING

OBJECTIVE:
To practice rebounding techniques while using a zone defense.

DESCRIPTION:
The drill involves two groups of three players. One group is on offense (O), while the other is on defense (X). The drill begins by having an offensive player on the point pass the ball to a player on the wing who shoots it. Once the shot has been taken, the defensive player covering the shooter drops back to the middle of the lane to create a triangle coverage of the foul lane rebounding area with the other two (X)s. The (X)s keep their hands up and attempt to keep any offensive player from penetrating the triangle area.

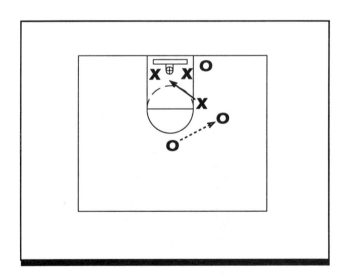

DRILL 64
1-3-1
ZONE DEFENSE WING

OBJECTIVE:
To teach defensive rebounding while playing a 1-3-1 or 1-2-2 zone defense.

DESCRIPTION:
The drill involves two groups of four players. One group plays offense (P-1 to P-4), while the other is on defense (X-1 to X-4). The drill begins with P-1 with a ball. P-1 passes to any offensive player. All offensive players can pass crosscourt—except P-3 and P-4 cannot pass to each other. P-3 and P-4 can pass to any other player. With a single exception, only P-1 and P-2 may shoot. If either P-3 or P-4 receives a crosscourt pass, they are permitted to shoot a lay-up. X-2 and X-3 attempt to intercept any crosscourt pass. They also must clear out on any attempted shot. P-1 and P-3 may throw lob passes, but they are not allowed to dribble or move.

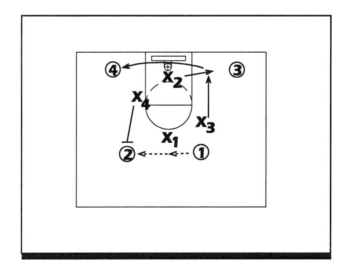

DRILL 65
TWO-ONE-TWO
INSIDE DEFENSE REBOUNDING

OBJECTIVE:
To teach rebounding positions to inside defenders; to practice sliding and rebounding techniques.

DESCRIPTION:
The drill involves ten players divided into two five-player teams. The teams engage in five-on-five competition. The drill begins with all players assuming a position as illustrated. One team is on offense (P-1 to P-5), while the other team is on defense (X-1 to X-5). The drill is conducted according to specific performance guidelines. P-1 and P-2 can shoot jump shots, drive to the basket, or pass to P-3 or P-4. P-5 can pass the ball in to either P-3 or P-4 who post up. P-1, P-2, and P-5 are required to hold the ball for a two count before passing or dribbling. Once the defensive players have mastered the necessary defensive slides (moves), the offensive players can pass the ball as quickly as they want. The emphasis for the defenders should be on hustling.

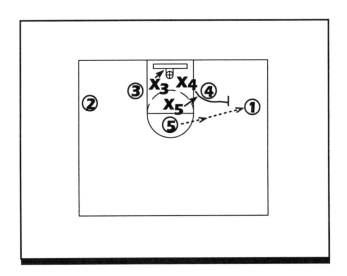

DRILL 66
TWO-BALL, WEAK SIDE WING

OBJECTIVE:
To practice defensive rebounding techniques and to develop stamina.

DESCRIPTION:
The drill involves five players—four on offense (P-1 to P-4) and one on defense (X).
The drill begins by having the coach (C) and P-3 pass the ball back and forth until (C)
throws a pass to P-4. (X) must deflect the pass to P-4. (C) then takes a second ball
(off the floor) and passes it to P-3. (X) quickly moves back out to cover P-3. In the
meantime, P-4 picks up the deflected pass and passes it back to (C). P-3 is given
two dribbles to attack (X). If P-3 is unable to score, the ball is passed back to the
(C) and the drill begins again. (X) attempts to keep P-3 from driving to the inside. If
P-3 shoots, (X) and P-3 aggressively battle for the rebound. If P-3 scores or (X) get
the rebound, the players rotate. P-3 to P-4, P-4 to X, and X to the end of the line.
The next player in line becomes the new P-3. The (C) can add variety to the drill by
shooting at any time. If this occurs, P-3, P-4, and (X) battle for the rebound. (X)
should attempt to rebound the weak side and block out P-4.

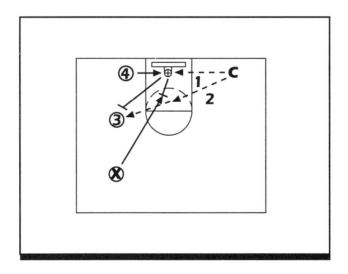

DRILL 67
TWO-BALL, STRONG SIDE WING

OBJECTIVE:
To teach defensive rebounding and to practice defensive slide movements.

DESCRIPTION:
The drill involves three players—two on offense (P-1 and P-2) and one on defense (X). The drill begins by having the coach (C) pass the ball back and forth to P-2, while (X) reacts as appropriate in the sliding movements of a one-two-two zone. (C) can also pass inside to P-1. If this occurs, (X) should deflect this pass. (C) then uses a second ball and passes to P-2. P-2 goes one-on-one against (X). P-2 is given two dribbles to score. If unable to do so, P-2 is required to pass back to (C). (X) should not allow P-2 to drive inside. At the same time, P-1 retrieves the deflected ball and either hands it to (C) or lays it at (C)'s feet. All the while, P-2 and (X) are engaged in one-on-one competition. P-1 then returns to the low-post position. The drill continues until P-2 shoots. The group then rotates.

VARIATION:
• Variety can be added to the drill by having (C) shoot. If (C) shoots, (X) must clear out P-2 before going for the rebound.

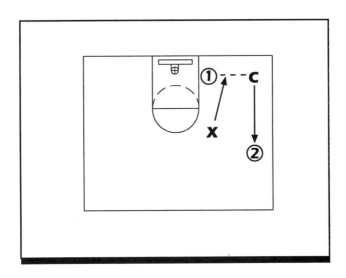

CHAPTER 7

PROGRESSION DRILLS

DRILL 68
JUST ONE-ON-ONE

OBJECTIVE:
To practice offensive and defensive rebounding techniques.

DESCRIPTION:
The drill involves two pairs of players—the pairs competing against each other on a one-on-one basis in a predetermined area of the floor. Extra players line up outside the court adjacent to each pair. One member of the pair is on defense (X-1, X-3), while the other is on offense (P-1, P-3). The drill involves progressively removing certain restrictions on the players (e.g., the area P-1 and P-3 may use to score; the number of dribbles the offensive players can use; having the defenders—X-1 and X-3—keep their hands behind their backs; and having only one pair of players compete at a time). After X-1 and X-3 begin to effectively control P-1 and P-3, the restrictions are relaxed (e.g., removed one at a time). Players rotate from offense to defense.

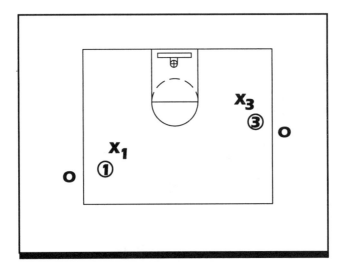

DRILL 69
DEFENSING THE SIDE AND LOW POST

OBJECTIVE:
To practice offensive and defensive rebounding techniques.

DESCRIPTION:
The drill involves four players at a time—three on offense (P-1, P-3, P-5) and one on defense (X-5). P-1 and P-3 line up on the side line, approximately 10-15 feet apart. X-5 defends P-5, either by fronting or standing behind P-5. The drill begins by having P-1 and P-3 pass the ball back and forth to each other until one of them can pass the ball to P-5. X-5 uses proper footwork to prevent P-5 from receiving the pass. Initially, P-5 is stationary. Once X-5 exhibits the proper footwork in relation to the position of the ball (which is being passed back and forth between P-1 and P-3), P-5 is permitted to slide up and down the lane in an attempt to get open for a pass. Once the pass is completed to P-5, P-5 goes one-on-one against X-5 and attempts to score. If the shot misses, X-5 boxes out and practices defensive rebounding techniques.

VARIATIONS:
- P-1 and P-3 can be allowed to shoot, causing both P-5 and X-5 to go to the boards.
- X-5 can be required to play in front or behind P-5.

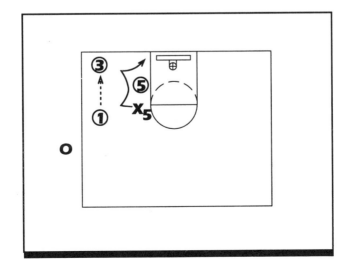

DRILL 70
DENY BALL REVERSAL AND DEFEND

OBJECTIVE:
To teach offensive and defensive rebounding techniques.

DESCRIPTION:
The drill involves four players. Players P-1 and X-1 go one-on-one against each other, with P-1 who has the ball on offense. Play starts near midcourt. X-1 vigorously defends against P-1. Initially, P-1 is permitted only two dribbles before having to pass the ball to either P-2 or P-3. P-1 is not permitted to take an obviously bad shot at any time. P-1 is also required to stay within the extended foul lane lines. As soon as P-1 can get open after passing the ball, P-1 receives a return pass from the player who received the pass. In the initial stages of the drill, P-1 is restricted to shooting a lay-up. As the drill (or season) progresses, jump shots are permitted. X-1 attempts to deny all passes. Once the shot is taken, X-1 blocks out P-1 and goes for the rebound. The drill continues until X-1 steals or rebounds the ball or P-1 scores.

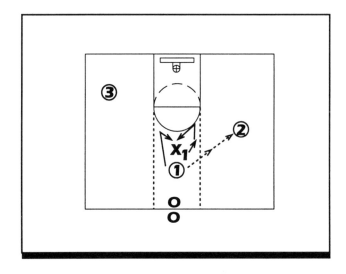

DRILL 71
ONE-ON-ONE HALF COURT,
MULTIPLE DEFENSIVE MANEUVERS

OBJECTIVE:
To teach offensive rebounding techniques.

DESCRIPTION:
The players form a single line facing the basket. The first two players in the line (X-1 and X-2) engage in one-on-one competition. X-2 has the ball; X-1 is defending. If X-2 scores, X-1 takes the ball out-of-bounds and passes it to X-3 (the next player in line). X-2 then becomes the defender against X-3, using denial, face-ground, and other assorted moves. X-3 attempts to score. If X-2 misses the shot against X-1, X-1 blocks out X-2 from the boards, rebounds the ball, and throws an outlet pass to X-3, simulating a fast break. X-3 receives the pass and then goes on the attack against X-2. X-1 goes to the end of the line, and the drill continues.

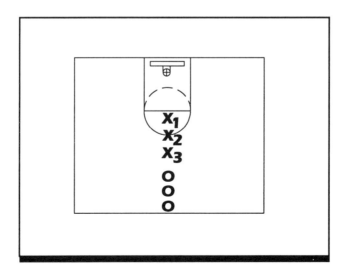

DRILL 72
TWO-BALL REBOUNDING

OBJECTIVE:
To teach rebounders to make a continuous effort to go for the ball; to practice both clearing-out and rebounding techniques.

DESCRIPTION:
The drill involves three-on-three competition between offensive players (O) and defensive players (X). The drill begins by having the coach (C) shoot a ball. As soon as the (X)s control the rebound of that shot, the manager (M) shoots a second ball. Both the (X)s and the (O)s aggressively attempt to rebound both shots. The (X)s outlet each rebound they retrieve to the (C) or (M). Offensive rebounds are put back up by the (O)s. Once a shot is made by the (O)s, the drill stops.

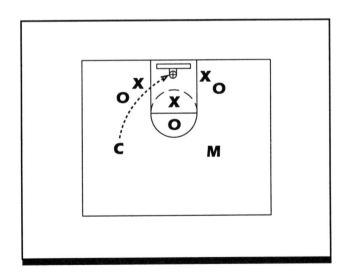

DRILL 73
SEMI-CIRCLE REBOUNDING

OBJECTIVE:
To practice rebounding techniques, defensive skills, and passing skills.

DESCRIPTION:
The drill involves seven players—six offensive players who form a semi-circle (O-1 through O-6) and a defensive player (X-1). The drill begins by having the coach (C) pass to any offensive player who is on the opposite side of the court from X-1. X-1 is assigned to guard an offensive player (in this instance O-1). When (C) passes the ball, O-1 cuts to the ball, going either in front of or behind X-1. X-1 defenses O-1. X-1 tries to keep O-1 in front of X-1 and to prevent O-1 from cutting behind X-1. X-1 also tries to beat O-1 to the designated spot. If X-1 beats O-1 to the spot, thereby preventing O-5 from making a pass to O-1, O-5 shoots the ball. X-1 and O-1 then go for the rebound. If X-1 does not beat O-1 to the spot, then O-5 passes to O-1. At that point, O-1 and X-1 go one-on-one. Play continues until either O-1 scores or X-1 gets the ball (by stealing or rebounding it).

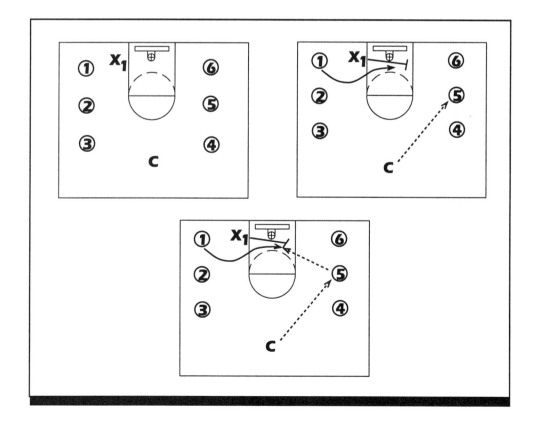

DRILL 74
INSIDE DEFENSE AGAINST
CONTINUOUS MOVEMENT

OBJECTIVE:
To practice inside defensive techniques and to teach offensive and defensive re-bounding skills.

DESCRIPTION:
The drill involves nine players—three as perimeter passers (P), three as offensive players (X), and three as defenders (D). The drill begins by having the three (P)s pass the ball to each other while looking for an (O) who is open to receive a pass. The three (O)s can move in any direction they want. They can screen for each other, roll back to the ball, flash pivot, or do any other move to get open, but they cannot move more than a step outside the paint (area). The (X)s attempt to keep the (O)s from receiving a pass from the (P)s. If the (O)s receive a pass, the (X)s defend against a shot or another penetrating pass. Once they have the ball, if the (O)s don't like their potential shot, the ball is passed back out to the (P)s and the drill (movement) continues. If the (O)s shoot, both the (O)s and the (X)s attack the board in an attempt to get the rebound. The (X)s clear out before going for the rebound. If the (O)s score or the (X)s rebound, the drill stops and the players rotate—the (X)s go to the end of the line, the (O)s become the new defenders, the (P)s become the new (O)s , and the first three players in line become the new (P)s.

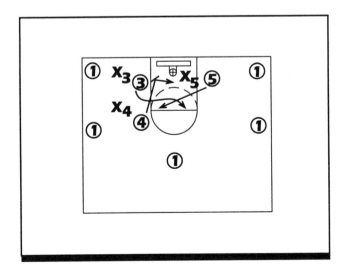

DRILL 75
FIVE-ON-FIVE DEFENSE GAME

OBJECTIVE:

To practice rebounding techniques and to develop a sense of team play.

DESCRIPTION:

Two five-person teams engage in five-on-five half-court competition. One team is on defense (O), while the other team remains on offense (X) until one team scores six points. The scoring system used is as follows: one point for each defensive rebound, turn-over, basket, being fouled, or passing (or dribbling) the ball into the point area; and two points for an offensive rebound.

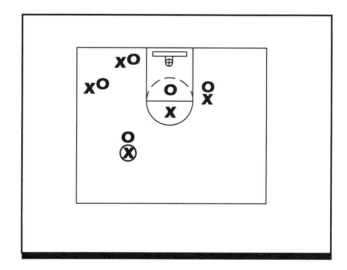

DRILL 76
DEFENDING THE SIDE AND LOW POST

OBJECTIVE:
To practice rebounding techniques and transitional patterns.

DESCRIPTION:
The drill involves five defensive players. Four players line up on the free throw lanes (two on each side). One player assumes a position several feet in front of the top of the key. The drill is initiated by having the coach (C) shoot a free throw. One of the two inside players rebounds the missed shot and throws an outlet pass to the nearest player who has moved to the wing to receive the pass. The off guard takes the center lane. The guard who is boxing out the shooter (C) takes the opposite side lane. After the outlet pass has been made, the three guards transition into a fast break. New guards take the place of the players who participated in the fast break, while the forwards either switch sides or are replaced by new players.

COACHING POINTS:
- The drill can also be conducted from out-of-bounds after a successful free throw.
- Two or more opposing players (up to five) can be added to increase the pressure on the five members of the rebounding group.
- Proper boxing-out techniques and movement patterns should be emphasized.

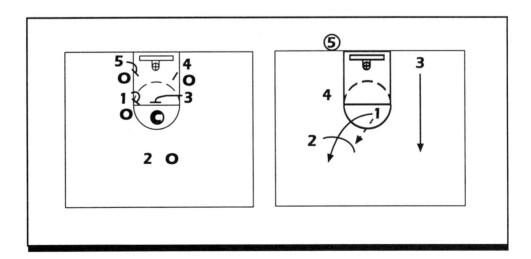

DRILL 77
INTERCEPT

OBJECTIVE:
To teach players to transit quickly from offense to a pressing defense.

DESCRIPTION:
The drill involves five players. The drill begins by having the players run an offensive play. One of the players shoots. As the shot leaves the shooter's hand, two players go to a safety defensive position, while the other three crash the boards looking for an offensive rebound. After the basket is made, the five players all quickly assume their positions in a pressing defense. The coach (C) then grabs the ball out of the net and tosses a semi-lob baseball pass into the defenders' area. A defender intercepts the ball and passes it to a teammate in front of the intercepter. The teammates then fill the lanes, take the ball up the court, and turn the interception into a score. The defenders then hustle back to their respective positions in the defensive press, and the drill continues.

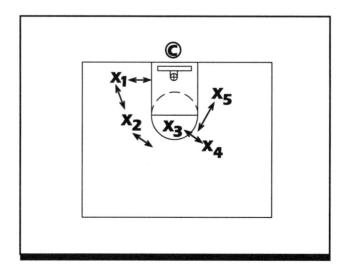

DRILL 78
FIVE-ON-FIVE WITH REBOUNDER

OBJECTIVE:
To have defenders practice proper player-to-player defensive and rebounding techniques, while offensive team members practice player-to-player offensive skills and offensive rebounding techniques.

DESCRIPTION:
The drill involves ten players—five on offense and five on defense. A rebounder ring over the rim is used so that no shot can be made. The offense runs a play designated by the coach, against an aggressive player-to-player defense. The offense shoots at the first opportunity. Both teams go strongly for the rebound. If the defenders get the rebound, they become the offensive team. If the offensive team gets the rebound, they continue on offense again. If a jump ball results, the defenders become the offensive team. The first team to score a preset number of points wins.

COACHING POINTS:
- The offense must run the designated play.
- The elimination of offensive turnovers should be emphasized.
- The defenders must use only player-to-player defensive techniques.
- Any violations of "rules" can be penalized by deducting points.

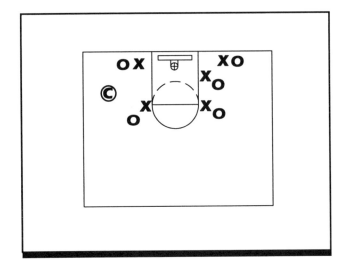

DRILL 79
THREE-ON-THREE STATIONARY

OBJECTIVE:
To practice passing, screening, clearing-out, and rebounding techniques.

DESCRIPTION:
The players form three lines. The drill involves six players—three on defense (X) and three on offense (O). The drill begins by having the three (O)s pass the ball to each other. After making three passes, (O) shoots the ball. The (X)s immediately block out, while the (O)s attempt to get to the ball to rebound it. If the (O)s get the rebound, they pass the ball another three times before shooting it again. If the (X)s rebound the ball, the drill ends and the players rotate. The (X)s go to the end of the line, while the (O)s become the new defenders. The next player in each line then goes on offense.

COACHING POINTS:
- The coach should have the defensive players focus on reacting quickly to the need to clear out.
- The drill can be varied by having the offensive players shoot on the coach's command instead of after the third pass, or begin the drill each time from a different spot on the court.

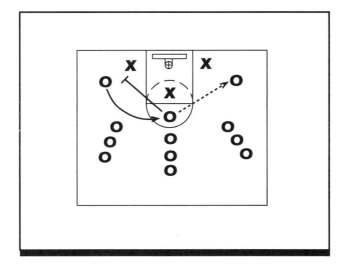

DRILL 80
THREE-ON-THREE CLOSE-OUT
AND CLEAR-OUT

OBJECTIVE:
To practice offensive and defensive rebounding techniques, clearing-out moves, out-let passing, and transitional footwork.

DESCRIPTION:
The drill involves three-on-three competition at each end of the court. The drill in-volves "make-it, take-it" competition, wherein the drill is only restarted after a shot is made. If the offensive players (O) get the rebound, play continues unchanged. If the defensive players (X) get the rebound, they outlet the ball past the top-of-the-key area—whereupon the (O)s and (X)s switch roles and play continues. The drill goes on for either a predetermined length of time or until one group makes a preset number of shots.

COACHING POINTS:
- The coach should have the (O)s aggressively work to get open for a shot.
- The coach should have both groups utilize proper rebounding mechanics.
- The rebounders should be required to capture the ball with both hands.
- The (X)s should use a front turn before outletting the ball above the free throw line.

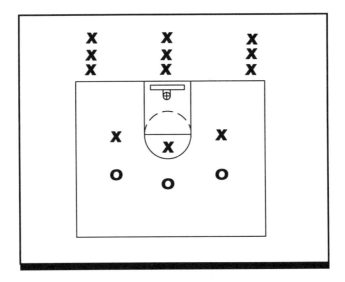

DRILL 81
FIVE-ON-FIVE BLOCK OFF

OBJECTIVE:
To practice clearing out, rebounding techniques, and outlet passing.

DESCRIPTION:
The drill involves two five-player teams engaged in five-on-five competition. One team is on offense (P-1 to P-5), while the other is on defense (X-1 to X-5). The drill begins with P-1 with a ball. P-1 either shoots or passes to P-2 who then shoots. After the shot is taken, X-3 and X-5 use either an inside or a reverse method to clear out P-3 and P-5. X-4 blocks the path of P-4. X-1 and X-2 use a "clear-and-go" technique to brush their opponents and then release to an outlet area to be prepared to start a fast break.

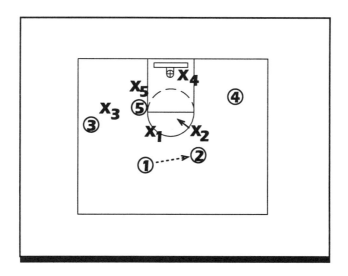

CHAPTER 8

AGGRESSIVENESS DRILLS

DRILL 82
BURST-OUT

OBJECTIVE:
To practice rebounding aggressively while using proper clearing-out and rebounding techniques.

DESCRIPTION:
The drill involves three players—one shooter (P-1), one defensive rebounder (X) and one offensive rebounder (O). P-1 shoots the ball, which is then rebounded by (X). (X) then fights (dribbles) through a double-team set by P-1 and (O). (X) keeps relatively low while dribbling. The drill can be conducted by having the players either rotate positions or set up in a line behind P-1 and rotate from the line into the drill.

COACHING POINTS:
- The defensive players should use proper rebounding techniques at all times.
- The rebounders should protect ball at all costs.

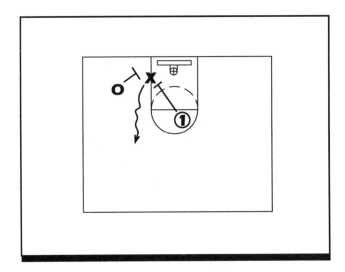

DRILL 83
AGGRESSIVE REBOUNDING

OBJECTIVE:
To increase aggressiveness while rebounding and to develop the ability to withstand the contact and pressure which occurs during rebounding.

DESCRIPTION:
The players form three lines. The first player in each line competes against the first player in the other two lines. The three competing players assume a position in front of and facing the basket. The drill begins by having the coach (C) toss the ball off the backboard. All three players compete for the rebound. The player getting the rebound becomes the offensive player and attempts to score against the other two players who then go on defense. Once a score is made, the drill is repeated with the same three players until one player scores two baskets. If an offensive player misses the shot and the ball stays in the lane, the player getting the rebound then goes on offense against the other two players. Once a player scores twice, that player goes to the end of that player's line. The first group of players in a line to get all of the players through is the winner. On a made shot or a ball that rebounds outside the lane area, the ball goes back to the (C) and the drill is repeated.

COACHING POINTS:
- Players should be encouraged to play with intensity and aggressiveness.
- Physical contact should be ignored.
- All shots should be put back up aggressively—not with finesse.
- Players should keep their hands up.

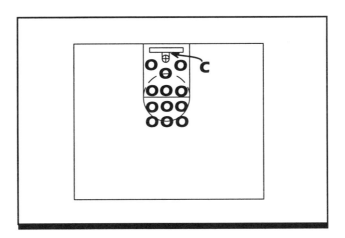

DRILL 84
MISSING BALL

OBJECTIVE:
To develop player aggressiveness and to practice rebounding techniques.

DESCRIPTION:
The drill involves three two-player teams (P-1 and P-4; P-2 and P-5; and P-3 and P-6). The drill is initiated with players P-1 and P-3 positioned on the wing adjacent to the free throw line. Both P-1 and P-3 have a basketball. P-2 assumes a position in front of the basket. The drill begins by having both P-1 and P-3 shoot the ball. If the shooter makes the shot, the shooter passes the ball back to the shooter's teammate who then shoots. As long as a pair of players (team) keeps scoring, they retain the ball. If the shooter misses the shot, both the shooter and P-2 go for the rebound. If the shooter gets the rebound, the ball is again passed back to the shooter's teammate and the drill continues as before. If P-2 gets the rebound, the ball is passed to P-5 who then shoots. The shooter who lost the rebound remains in the middle waiting for the next missed shot. The first pair to score a preset number of baskets (e.g., 15) wins.

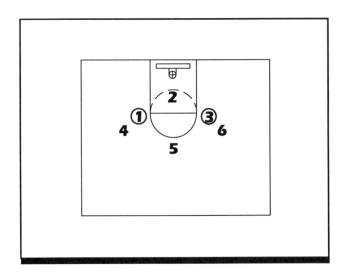

DRILL 85
THREE-ON-THREE, NO-HOLDS-BARRED FULL-COURT

OBJECTIVE:
To develop aggressiveness and to practice rebounding techniques.

DESCRIPTION:
The players form three lines outside the far court. The first player in each line participates in a three-person team (X) which brings the ball up the court and attempts to score against two defenders (O). After taking the three-on-two fast-break shot, the (X)s continue to rebound the ball as many times as they can recover the ball—after both made and missed shots. Once either (X) gets the ball, the (O)s attempt to prevent the (X)s from taking (moving) the ball back up the court. The drill is conducted in an aggressive, "no-holds-barred" manner. The coach can enhance the competitiveness of the drill by counting the number of rebounds a three-person group scores. Highest score during the entire drill wins the competition.

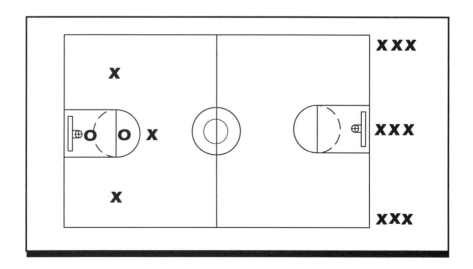

DRILL 86
THREE-ON-THREE ROUND-ROBIN

OBJECTIVE:
To improve rebounding intensity and to practice rebounding techniques.

DESCRIPTION:
The players are divided into three-person teams, which compete against each other—two at a time—in a round-robin schedule. One of the competing teams begins the drill on defense (X), while the other starts in an offensive position (O). The coach (C) takes a shot, and both teams vie for the rebound. The team getting the rebound is awarded a point. The teams alternate offense and defense so that neither team has the advantage of inside position. A game consists of one team scoring five points. If the score is tied at four points each, all six players start the drill side-by-side in the lane to prevent either team from having an advantage during the deciding point. The round-robin schedule can be used to manipulate the competition to fit the situation.

COACHING POINTS:
- All players should seal out properly.
- Contact is permitted (indeed encouraged).
- All rebounds are live until the whistle is blown.
- Play may occur anywhere on the court.

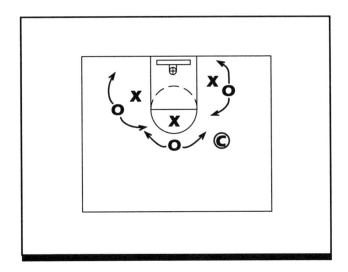

DRILL 87
BATTLE TIME

OBJECTIVE:
To develop aggressiveness and to practice rebounding techniques.

DESCRIPTION:
Players divide into groups of 4-8 at each basket, with three players in the game at one time. Extra players may shoot free throws until they're rotated into the game. The drill begins by having the coach shoot the ball and miss (either intentionally or as a result of using a big ball). The coach (C) also serves as a possible passing outlet for the rebounder. The three players in the game aggressively go for the rebound. The player who gets the rebound goes on offense, while the other two become defenders. The offensive player attempts to score using whatever moves necessary. All shots must be taken in the free throw lane. The rebounder may outlet the ball to (C) and get open for a return pass. Only major fouls are called. Play has no boundary except for where the shots can be taken. Three shots made allows a player to rotate out of the drill. (Note: The other two players retain their totals as the drill is continued with a new player participating.)

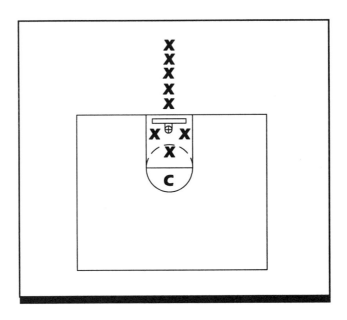

DRILL 88
FOUR-ON-FOUR TIME

OBJECTIVE:
To develop aggressiveness and to practice rebounding techniques.

DESCRIPTION:
The players are assigned to four-player groups. Two groups engage in four-on-four competition—one foursome is on defense (X), while the other is on offense (O). The drill begins by having the coach (C) shoot the ball. Once the shot is taken, the defensive player nearest to (C) yells "hands." All (X)s then clear out and go for the rebound. All (O)s also attempt to get the rebound. If the (X)s rebound the ball, the drill stops and all players either rotate one position clockwise or counterclockwise or switch roles (offense to defense and vice versa). If the (O)s rebound the ball, the (O)s either attempt to take the ball back up or outlet pass it back to (C),   and the drill resumes.

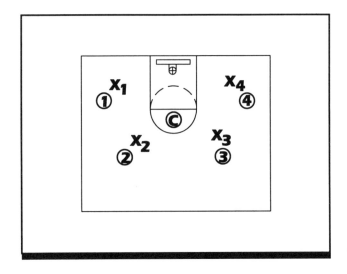

DRILL 89
FIVE-ON-FIVE RANDOM MOVEMENT

OBJECTIVE:
To practice rebounding techniques; to develop aggressiveness; and to work on foot-work.

DESCRIPTION:
The drill involves two five-person teams engaged in five-on-five competition. One team assumes an offensive role (O), while the other team is on defense. Two coaches (C) also participate in the drill. The drill begins either by having the (C)s pass the ball to each other before shooting (note: the players move and react to the relative position of the ball) or by having the (C)s pass the ball to one of the (O)s who is then required to shoot it. Once the shot is taken, both groups aggressively go for the rebound and each made shot.)

COACHING POINT:
*   If a squad had 15 players, the drill can be conducted with three teams of five players each.

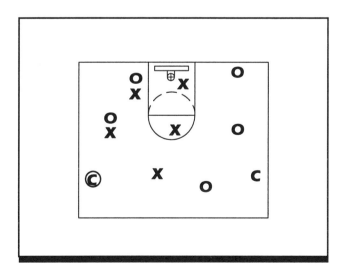

CHAPTER 9

STAMINA DRILLS

DRILL 90
NON-STOP TIPPING

OBJECTIVE:
To develop stamina; to practice tipping techniques; and to enhance hand-eye coordination.

DESCRIPTION:
The drill involves two players at a time. Each player tips his/her own rebound against the board continuously for a predetermined number of repetitions or a preset length of time. Once that point is reached, the players interchange sides.

VARIATIONS:
- The players should initially use either hand to tip, then the hand corresponding to the side on which they're tipping.
- The players should alternate in non-stop fashion a preset number of tips (e.g., five) with a preset number of conditioning, calisthenic-type exercises (e.g., squat thrusts, push-ups, etc.)

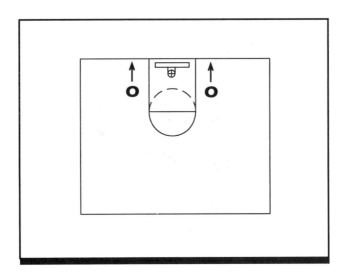

DRILL 91
OVER-AND-BACK TAPPING

OBJECTIVE:
To develop stamina and to practice timing and quick jumping.

DESCRIPTION:
The drill involves two players at a time. The two players line up facing the basket on opposite sides of the foul lane. The drill commences by having one player tap the ball over the basket to the other player. They then continue to tap the ball back and forth to each other for a preset number of times or a predetermined period of time. If they allow the ball to hit the floor, the drill (and the count) begins again.

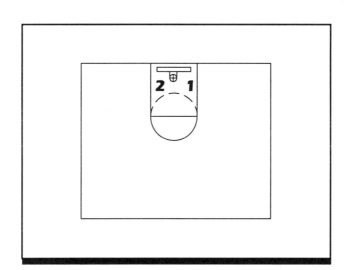

DRILL 92
TRAILER-AND-REBOUND

OBJECTIVE:
To develop stamina and to practice speed dribbling, rebounding skills, and outletting techniques.

DESCRIPTION:
The drill involves having the players divide into pairs. Each pair is given a basketball. One player is given the ball, while the other player acts. All of the pairs line up on the baseline. The drill begins by having the player with the ball speed dribble the length of the court and attempt a lay-in. After the shot, the shooter continues on to the outlet spot. The trailer who followed the shooter down the court then rebounds the ball and makes an outlet pass to the original shooter. That player again drives the length of the floor to shoot another lay-up at the opposite basket. The trailer then rebounds again. The next time through the drill, the players switch their roles.

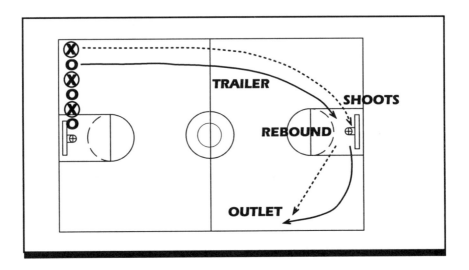

DRILL 93
THREE-MAN FULL-COURT

OBJECTIVE:
To develop stamina and to practice rebounding techniques and shooting three-point shots.

DESCRIPTION:
The players are divided into three-player groups. The drill begins with one group of players (P-1, P-2, P-3) participating. P-1 speed dribbles the length of the court to the other end and shoots a shot from three-point range. All three players fight for the rebound. Whichever player gets the rebound speed dribbles back to the opposite end of the court, followed by the other two players. Once the ball crosses half-court, the next group of players (P-4, P-5, P-6) begin the drill. The first group continues on the basket also. The dribbler then shoots from three-point range, and all three players go for the rebound. The drill continues until a set number of points are scored. (Note: One point can be awarded for each shot made and for each rebound.)

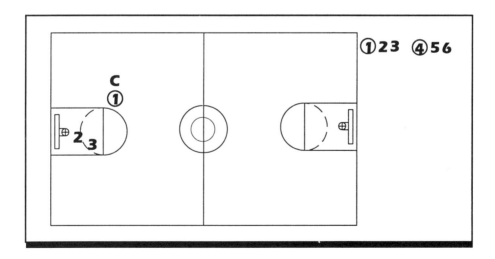

DRILL 94
REBOUND, SPRINT, QUICK FEET

OBJECTIVE:
To develop stamina and to practice selected offensive rebounding techniques.

DESCRIPTION:
The drill involves six players initially—three offensive (X) and three defensive (O). The defensive players try (half-heartedly) to box-out the (X)s, but eventually let the (X)s beat them. The three (X)s then use one of the following techniques for offensive rebounding.

- "Step and go" (also referred to as the swim technique)—where players step and fake in one direction, but quickly move in another direction to the basket.
- "Spin"—the (X)s attack the (O)s feet and spin the (O)s around, using either foot as a pivot foot.
- "Hook step"—(X)s lock feet with an (O) in order to be on the same standing as the (O).

The two offensive wing players jump and touch the backboard as high as they can five times. The center offensive player touches the rim five times. All three offensive players then sprint to the free throw line on the opposite end of the court, turn, face defense, and perform 10 seconds of quick feet. At the point, the players rotate: the (X)s go off the floor; the (O)s become (X)s; and three new players come on as (O)s.

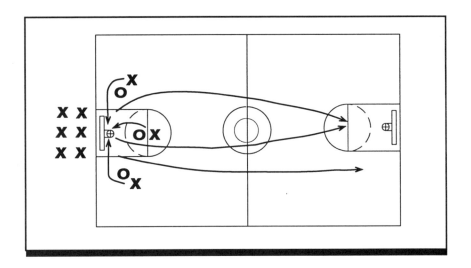

DRILL 95
PRESSURE COOKER

OBJECTIVE:
To develop stamina and to practice rebounding techniques when playing a full-court pressure defense.

DESCRIPTION:
The drill involves six players. Two players (X)s, assume a defensive position, line up at the top of the free throw circle facing the four offensive players (O) who are spaced equidistant down the sideline the full length of the court. The (O) closest to the (X)s has a basketball. That player then passes the ball to the next player in line and so on until the ball reaches the corner (last) player, who then shoots the ball. The shooter and the last player making a pass go to the boards to attempt a rebound. In the meantime, the two (X)s sprint down the court as soon as the first pass is made. One (X) blocks out the shooter, while the other (X) blocks out the passer. The decision regarding which (X) blocks out which (O) is made between the two (X)s. Similar to the (O)s, the (X)s attempt to rebound the shot. Whichever team is successful in rebounding goes off the court and is replaced by new players. Whichever twosome is unsuccessful goes again.

COACHING POINTS:
- The players should be taught to go to the weak side board by requiring that one (X) always goes opposite when the shot is attempted; while the other (X) blocks out the closest player to the ball.
- The (X)s should not be allowed to leave their initial positions until after the first pass is thrown.
- The (X)s should face the basket at the end of the floor where they begin the drill.
- The (O) shooter should shoot from 15-20 feet.
- Using proper clear-out techniques and going strongly for the ball should be stressed.

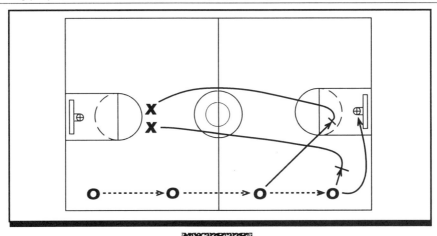

DRILL 96
POWER SLIDE

OBJECTIVE:
To develop stamina, explosiveness and shooting the ball using a power move.

DESCRIPTION:
The drill involves one player at a time using two basketballs. The player (P-3) as-sumes a position facing the basket in the foul lane in front of the circle. The two balls are placed on the floor adjacent to P-3 outside the foul line. The drill begins by having P-3 slide to the ball on the left and shoot it. P-3 then slides back to the ball on the right and uses an explosive power move to shoot a lay-up. Players P-1 and P-2 replace the basketballs shot by P-3, and the drill continues for a preset number of repetitions or length of time.

VARIATION:
• Instead of having P-3 pick the basketballs off the floor, P-1 and P-2 could either pass the ball to P-3 or throw the ball off the backboard for P-3 to retrieve.

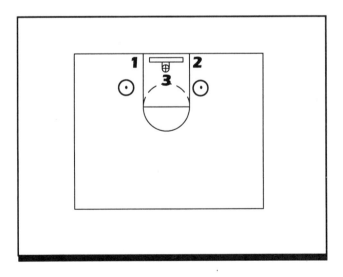

DRILL 97
TWO-BALL, BASELINE

OBJECTIVE:
To develop stamina and to practice defensive rebounding techniques.

DESCRIPTION:
The drill involves five players —four offense (P-1 to P-4) and one on defense (X). The drill begins by having the coach (C) and P-3 pass the ball back and forth. At some point, (C) passes inside to P-4. (X) deflects this pass. Using a second ball, (C) immediately passes to P-3. (X) hustles out to cover P-3. P-4 retrieves the deflected ball and passes it back either to (C) or to a manager (M) who gives it to (C). After receiving the pass, P-3 goes one-on-one against (X). (X) attempts to keep P-3 from driving to the baseline. P-3 is limited to two dribbles. If P-3 does not shoot within two dribbles, the ball is passed out to (C). (C) then passes again to P-4 and the drill continues as before. Variety can be added to the drill by having (C) shoot. If this occurs, (X) must clear out P-4 before going for the rebound. The drill can be made further competitive by requiring that P-3 or P-4 replace (X), if (X) stops either P-3's or P-4's one-on-one move.

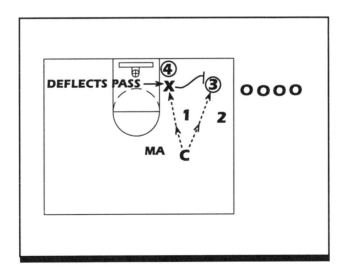

DRILL 98
NON-STOP INTENSITY

OBJECTIVE:
To develop stamina and to practice putting the ball back up.

DESCRIPTION:
The players form two lines. The first player in each line participates in the drill. The two players (X and O) line up side by side in the lane. The drill begins by having a third player (P-3) shoot the ball from the free throw line. (X) and (O) then fight for the rebound and put the ball back up. Even if the shot is made, they grab the ball out of the net and put it back up. Regardless of whether they make or miss the shot, (X) and (O) continue to rebound and shoot the ball back up on a non-stop basis for a predetermined length of time (e.g., one minute). If the ball bounces out of the lane area, the player retrieving the ball quickly throws it back to P-3 who immediately shoots it again. A reasonable amount of contact is allowed during the drill. The drill continues for a set period of time per pair of players. The winning player between the two is the player who makes the most baskets. The winning team is the team that has the most winning players.

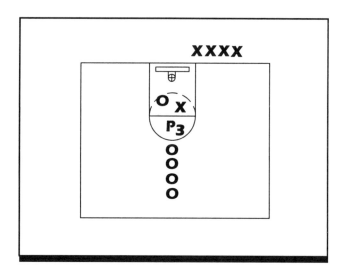

DRILL 99
SUPER CHALLENGE

OBJECTIVE:
To develop stamina and movement skills and to practice footwork and rebounding techniques.

DESCRIPTION:
The drill involves one player with a basketball. The player assumes a position facing the basket, midway down the outside of the foul lane area. The drill is initiated by having the player throw the ball off the backboard so that it carries to the opposite side of the lane. The player must reach the ball and rebound it before it hits the floor. The movement techniques across the lane should be a quick slide. The feet should never cross during the movement. The drill is continuous for a preset period of time.

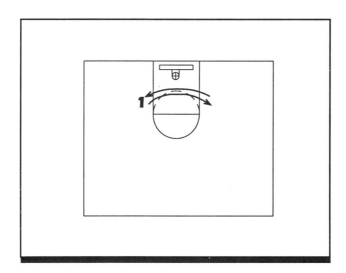

DRILL 100
TEAM FULL-COURT TAP

OBJECTIVE:
To develop stamina and to practice tapping techniques.

DESCRIPTION:
The players form two lines—with one line facing each basket. The first player in each line throws the ball up on the backboard and taps it back up high on the board. Following the tap, the player runs to the end of the opposite line. The next player continues the drill by another tap. Players in both lines continue tapping the balls (one at each basket). The drill is continued for a set period of time, with each player not letting the ball hit the floor. If the ball hits the floor, the drill is restarted.

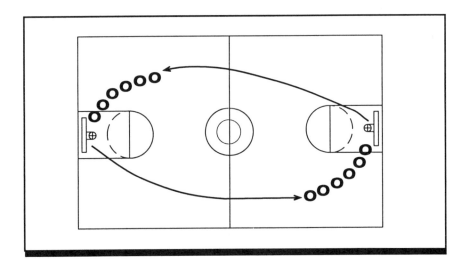

DRILL 101
FULL-COURT REBOUNDING RELAY

OBJECTIVE:
To develop stamina and to practice rebounding techniques, outlet passes, and pushing the ball up the court under control.

DESCRIPTION:
The players divide into three lines. The first player in each line (P-1, P-2, P-3) is given a ball and assumes a position on the court in front of the basket. Two coaches stand at mid-court on the sidelines. The drill begins by having P-1, P-2, and P-3 simultaneously throw the ball up on the backboard five times each—rebounding their own ball each time. After the fifth rebound, the player outlets the ball to an open coach (C). (C) throws the ball back to the player who then dribbles it to the opposite basket and repeats the five-toss-on-the-backboard, five-rebound process. After the fifth rebound at the other end, the player again throws another outlet pass to an open (C). The player then sprints to half-court and receives a return pass from (C). The player dribbles to the initial end line and hands the ball to the next player in line. The relay continues until every player on a team takes a turn. The first team finished wins the competition.

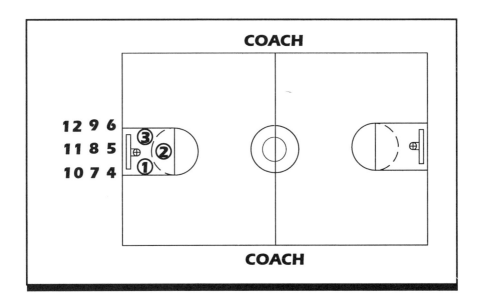

THE
AUTHORS

George Karl is the head coach of the Seattle SuperSonics. Since assuming his present position on January 23, 1992, Karl has led the Sonics to over 300 victories. In the process, Karl has the distinction of having achieved the highest winning percentage of any coach in Sonics histjory. Under Karl's tutelage, the Sonics have become one of the NBA's upper echelon teams. Twice, the Sonics have finished first in the NBA's Pacific Division, and in 1996, thay reached the NBA Finals. A 1973 graduate of North Carolina where he played three years for Dean Smith's Tar Heels and gained All-American honors as a senior, Karl began his distinguished coaching career in 1978 as an assistant in the ABA for the San Antonio Spurs. After two seasons with the Spurs, Karl then moved to the Continental Basketball Association as the head coach of the Montana Golden Nuggets. After three years with the Golden Nuggets, he began his NBA head coaching career with the Cleveland Cavaliers in 1984. Two years later, Karl accepted the same position with the Golden State Warriors—a job he held for two seasons. Subsequently, Karl spent two additional seasons each with the CBA's Albany Patroons and with Real Madrid of the Spanish League. One of the most respected and knowledgeable coaches in the game, Karl resides in the Seattle area with his wife Cathy and their two children—Kelci and Coby.

Terry Stotts is an assistant coach with the Seattle SuperSonics. He began his career with the Sonics in 1992 as a scout, before assuming his present position prior to the start of the 1993-94 season. In addition to his normal coaching duties, Stott's responsibilities include game preparation, coordinating NBA advance scouting, developing the Sonic defensive playbook and developing and coaching the Sonic forwards and centers. A 1980 graduate of the University of Oklahoma where he earned numerous honors as a basketball player for the Sooners, Stotts began his coaching career in 1990 as an assistant coach with the Albany Patroons under current Sonic head coach George Karl. He then spent one season as an assistant with the CBA's Fort Wayne Fury, before joining the Sonics staff. Terry and his wife Jan reside in the Seattle area.

Price Johnson is a successful youth basketball coach and basketball camp director in the Bellevue, Washington area. For the past 15 years, he has worked both as coach and as advocate of youth basketball. Since 1992, Johnson has taken an all-star youth basketball team to the national tournament for youth basketball, placing in the top 10 teams each year. Johnson has also done considerable volunteer work—serving on the Board of Directors of the Petaluma, California Boys and Girls Club working with the Boys and Girls Club of Bellevue, Washington and spending time assisting several high schools in the greater Seattle area. Johnson is a co-owner of Hoopaholics, a successful sportswear company. Price and his wife of 16 years, Julianne, reside in Bellevue, Washington with their two sons—James and Dane.

Terry Stotts, George Karl, Price Johnson (L-R)

ADDITIONAL BASKETBALL RESOURCES FROM

COACHES ≡ CHOICE

■ *101 DEFENSIVE BASKETBALL DRILLS*
by George Karl, Terry Stotts and Price Johnson
1997 ▪ Paper ▪ 128 pp
ISBN 1-57167-079-3 ▪ $15.00

■ *101 OFFENSIVE BASKETBALL DRILLS*
by George Karl, Terry Stotts and Price Johnson
1997 ▪ Paper ▪ 120 pp
ISBN 1-57167-078-5 ▪ $15.00

■ *101 BASKETBALL OUT-OF-BOUNDS DRILLS*
by George Karl, Terry Stotts and Price Johnson
1997 ▪ Paper ▪ 120 pp
ISBN 1-57167-099-8 ▪ $15.00

■ *101 WOMEN'S BASKETBALL DRILLS*
by Theresa Grentz and Gary Miller
1997 ▪ Paper ▪ 128 pp
ISBN 1-57167-083-1 ▪ $15.00

■ *ATTACKING ZONE DEFENSES*
by John Kresse and Richard Jablonski
1997 ▪ Paper ▪ 128 pp
ISBN 1-57167-047-5 ▪ $15.00